EARLY

UKIYO-E MASTER
Okumura Masanobu

Robert Vergez

KODANSHA INTERNATIONAL LTD.
Tokyo, New York and San Francisco

To my mentor and best friend Charles H. Mitchell

Note to the Reader: Japanese names in the text are given in the customary Japanese order, surname preceding given name.

Unnumbered Illustrations
Half-title page: *Tying the Sock.* 1750s. Large *ōban benizuri-e.* Ōta Memorial Museum of Art.
Title page: *Shusui Sanshoku.* 1710s. *Ōban sumizuri-e* with hand-coloring. Asahina Saburō, the mythical Hercules of Japan, and two youths admire the contents of an outsized sake cup. Author's collection.
Copyright page: *Sugoroku.* 1750s. *Hosoban benizuri-e.* A youth and a girl play a game similar to backgammon, while Hotei, one of the seven gods of happiness, referees the match.
Contents page: *Equestrian Feat.* 1740s. *Hashira-e* with hand-coloring. A Korean nobleman practicing calligraphy on horseback. Riccar Art Museum.

Distributed in the United States by Kodansha International/USA Ltd., through Harper & Row, Publishers, Inc., 10 East 53rd Street, New York, New York 10022.

Published by Kodansha International Ltd., 2-2, Otowa 1-chome, Bunkyo-ku, Tokyo 112 and Kodansha International/USA Ltd., 10 East 53rd Street, New York, New York 10022 and 44 Montgomery Street, San Francisco, California 94104.

copyright © 1983 by Kodansha International Ltd.
all rights reserved
printed in Japan
first edition, 1983
LCC 82-48780
ISBN 0-87011-587-1 (U.S.)
ISBN 4-7700-1087-7 (in Japan)

Library of Congress Cataloging in Publication Data
Vergez, Robert, 1924–
  Early ukiyo-e master, Okumura Masanobu.

  (Great Japanese Art series)
  1. Okumura, Masanobu, 1686–1764. 2. Ukiyoe.
I. Okumura, Masanobu, 1686–1764. II. Title.
III. Series.
NE1325.038V47   1983   769.92′4   82-48780
ISBN 0-87011-587-1 (U.S.)

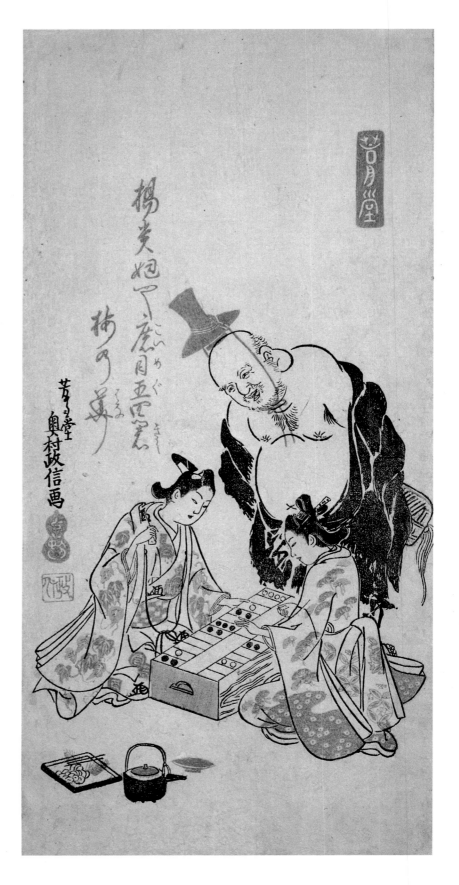

CONTENTS

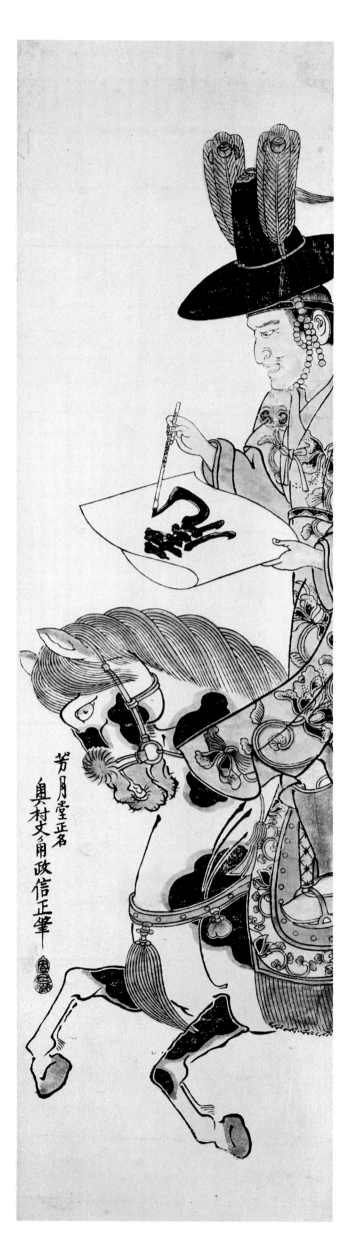

1. *Three Courtesans.*

2. *A Courtesan Standing.*

3. *A Courtesan Seated.*

奥
村
政
信
圖

5. An Iroko.

6. The Actor Ogino Isaburō.

大和画工

奥村政信筆

7. *Actor in the Role of Oshichi.*

8. *The Actor Ichikawa Danjūrō II.*

9. *The Actor Ichikawa Danjūrō II.*

10. *Onnagata in Snow.*

11. *A Beautiful Woman Strolling.*

12. *The Actor Tomisawa Montarō.*

13. *The Moon of Musashi.*

14. *Sparrows in the Snow.*

15. *A Paragon of Filial Piety.*

16. *Lovers Watching a Handsome Youth Write.*

17. *Teahouse Scene.*

18. *Enjoying the Evening Cool.*

19. *Main Entrance to the Yoshiwara.*

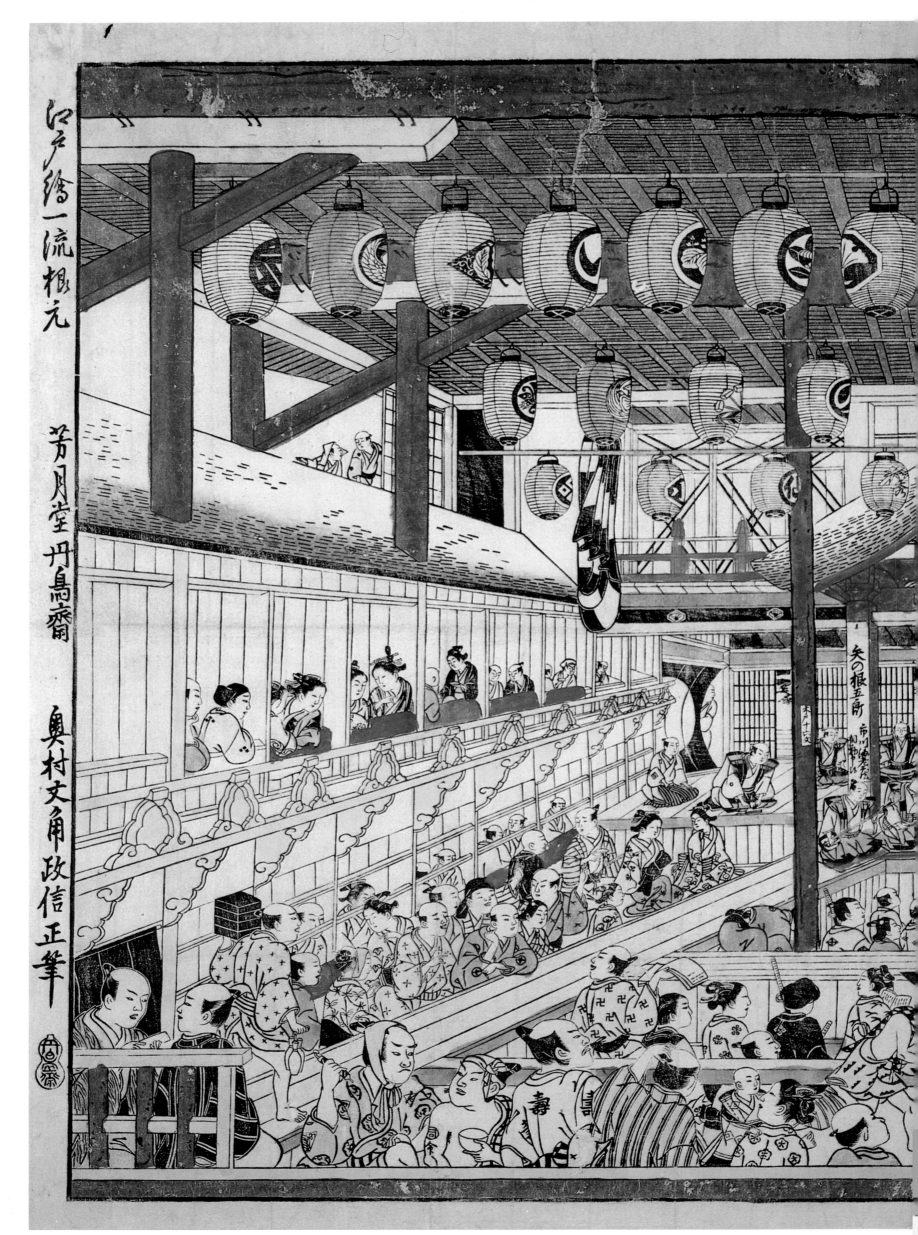

20. *Interior View of a Theater.*

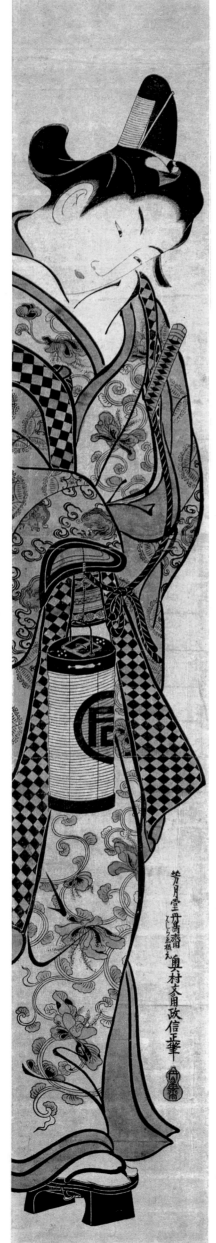

22. *Courtesan and Attendant.*

21. *The Actor Sanokawa Ichimatsu I.*

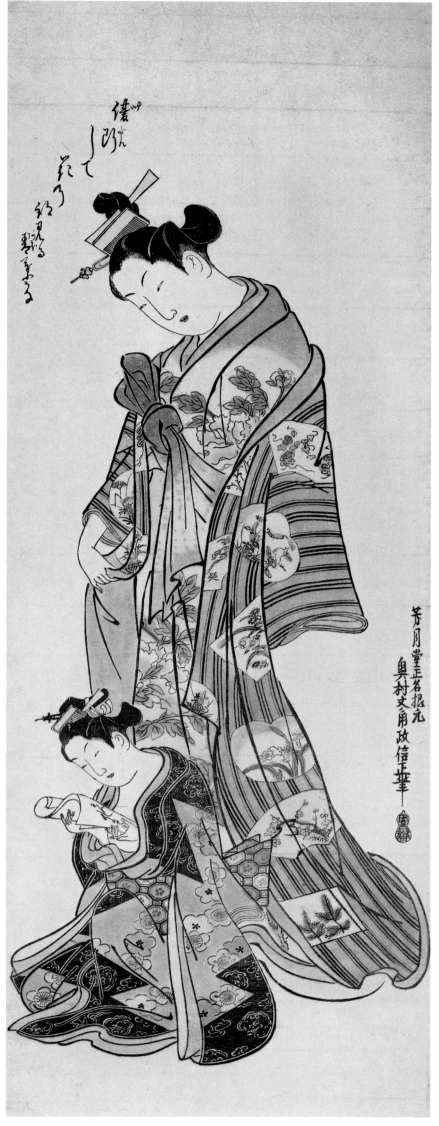

23. *Courtesan and Attendant.*

24. *Courtesan and Attendant.*

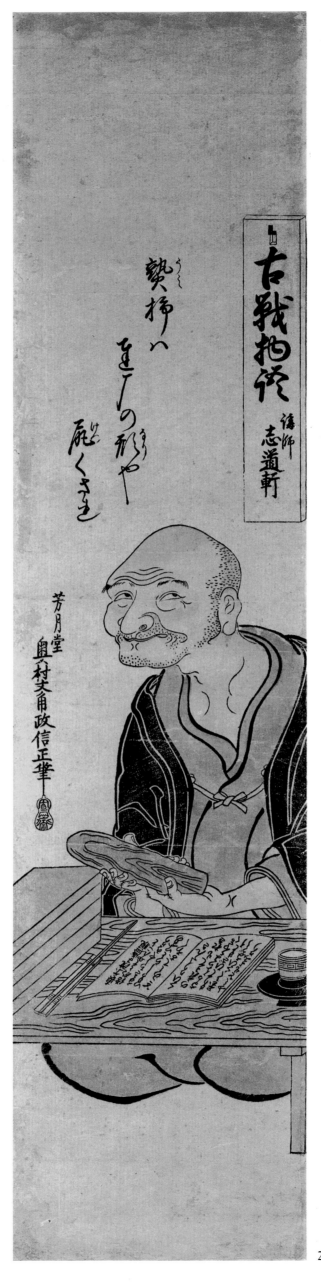

25. *Portrait of Shidōken.*

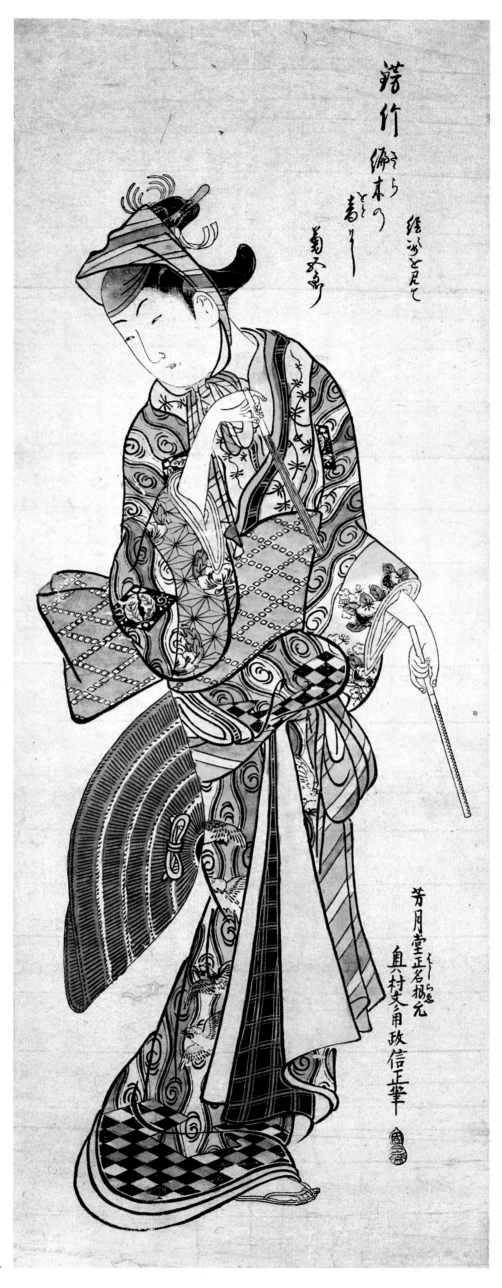

26. *The Actor Onoe Kikugorō I.*

尾
ガ
軒
乃
宀
イ
キ
ャ
ン
屋
ウ
屋
ヤ
杜
鵑

芳
月
堂
正
名

奥
村
文
角
政
信
正
筆

28. *A Gust of Wind.*

29. *The Actor Onoe Kikugorō I as Sukeroku.*

30. *The Actor Nakamura Kiyozō as Shimano Okan.*

31. *Kabuki Scene.*

32. *After the Bath.*

33. *The Actor Takinaka Hidematsu.*

34. *Teahouse Girl and Client.*

35. *The Ogura Mountain Retreat.*

EARLY UKIYO-E MASTER: Okumura Masanobu

MASANOBU'S FORMATIVE YEARS: THE GENROKU EPOCH

Since the end of last century, Western critics such as Fenollosa, Ficke, and Michener have unanimously recognized the aesthetic qualities of Okumura Masanobu's work and singled him out as one of the supreme masters of the woodblock print. Similarly, Japanese scholars have always held Masanobu in the highest esteem, and distinguished connoisseurs such as Professors Takahashi and Shibui have long swelled the ranks of Masanobu admirers. It is curious indeed that such a critical consensus, coming from so many authorities, should produce so little familiarity with Okumura Masanobu on the part of the art-conscious public. For even though Masanobu's creations were, more often than not, the expression of a hedonistic ambience peculiar to the Edo period (1600–1868), they speak a graphic language that is universally understood. The appreciation of Masanobu's prints, far from being the exclusive preserve of ukiyo-e specialists, can be shared by anyone willing to participate in the thrilling and unending search for beauty.

Masanobu was, there is no doubt, one of the most original of the ukiyo-e artists. Not only did he make major contributions with his comic albums, the introduction of European perspective, and the invention of the pillar print, but he also pioneered in the development of the lacquer print and two-color print. The popularity of ukiyo-e depended on such stylistic and technical innovation throughout its history, but this was especially true of the period of Masanobu's activity, the first half of the eighteenth century. Ukiyo-e then was often on the verge of stagnation, and it was Masanobu, through hundreds of varied compositions, who supplied the regenerative force that kept the art of this period flourishing. Significantly, he is the only artist whose career in effect spans the entirety of this, the so-called primitive period (which ended in 1764), from the early black-and-white broadsheets, through the elegant hand-colored prints (large and small), all the way down to the delicate two-color prints which preceded the birth of the full-color "brocade" prints. Last but not least, Masanobu became in the 1720s a successful wholesale publisher, an unusual profession for an artist insofar as none of the great ukiyo-e masters before or after him pursued a business career in this field.

MASANOBU'S ORIGINS

Okumura Masanobu was born around 1686, presumably in Edo (now Tokyo), on the threshold of the so-called Genroku epoch, which covered specifically the Genroku era (1688–1704) and also, by common acceptance, the Hōei (1704–11) and Shōtoku (1711–16) eras. The word renaissance has been aptly applied to this epoch, for it brought forth the works of creative giants such as Matsuo Bashō, Ihara Saikaku, Ejima Kiseki, Chikamatsu Monzaemon, and Ogata Kōrin. "Genroku may be looked upon," wrote Sir George Sansom,[43*] "as the zenith of Tokugawa prosperity, and perhaps even the justification of feudal rule, for here was peace and plenty and a great flourishing of the arts—a happy society as human societies go."

Edo, that small village originally named Chiyoda, had mushroomed during its first century of existence into a bustling city of more than half a million. And it was in this city that Masanobu grew up, worked, prospered, and died. He may be justly called, at least spiritually, a true *Edokko* (native of Edo)—naturally endowed with wit and ingenuity, constantly experimenting and innovating, bending his artistic talent to the ephemeral tastes of the public, and proud of his accomplishments.

Little is known of Masanobu's long life and nothing about his parents or wife. The standard biographies of ukiyo-e artists give him only scant reference.[§] The *Zōho ukiyo-e ruikō* reports, with more or less accuracy, that Masanobu was a wholesale publisher by the name of Okumura Genroku[64] or Gempachi; his pseudonyms were Bunkaku, Kammyō,[+] Hōgetsudō, and Tanchōsai; his bookstore was located in Edo Tōri Shio-chō, and later in Tōri Abura-chō; he called himself *Nihon eshi* ("Japanese artist"; indicating that Masanobu considered himself in the mainstream of Japanese graphic art) and used a red gourd-shaped seal; from the Hōei (1704–11) to Kyōhō (1716–36) eras he did many fashionable lacquer prints (*urushi-e*); he was the originator of the perspective print (*uki-e*); and most of his late

prints were sold in triptychs and colored in rose-red (*beni*) and light green (*moegi*).

Yamazaki Yoshishige (1797–1863), in *Meiyo ōrai* ("Celebrities Almanac"), reveals that Masanobu died at the age of seventy-nine (seventy-eight by Western count) on the eleventh day of the second month of Meiwa 1 (1764), although Meiwa 5 (1768) has also been given as the year of his death.[45] Since the earliest signed work of Masanobu was published in 1701, it would appear that he was already working professionally as a designer at the tender age of fifteen. According to the Meiwa 5 date, Masanobu would have been eleven at the beginning of his career and, however precocious he was, that date seems quite unlikely. So until further evidence to the contrary is produced, we should give credence to the dates 1686–1764.

The ukiyo-e art critic Inoue Kazuo also supports the validity of these dates.[14] He arrives at the conclusion that Masanobu died in Meiwa 1 (1764) after examining the painting of a "beautiful woman" (*bijin*) portraying Mikawa Manzai, formerly owned by Kobayashi Bunshichi, and signed "Painted by Hōgetsudō Tanchōsai Okumura Bunkaku Masanobu at the age of seventy-two." According to Inoue, the woman's coiffure belongs definitely to the mid Hōreki era (1751–64), that is around 1757, and if Masanobu's age, as stated in the signature, was seventy-two at that time, it follows that the year of his death (seven years later at seventy-nine) was 1764.

THE FIRST PRINTS

As already mentioned, Masanobu's first signed work appeared in 1701, or more exactly, in the eighth month of Genroku 14. It is a print album of courtesans of the Yoshiwara gay quarter, published by Kurihara Chōemon and signed "Drawn by the Japanese artist Okumura Gempachi Masanobu." Following this work, ten months later, was another album of courtesans (fig. 1), published by Otera Chōbei. These albums, and his other early designs as well, show the strong influence of his contemporaries of the powerful Torii school. In fact, the first two albums are virtually a pastiche of a folding album (*orihon*) by Torii Kiyonobu known as *Keisei ehon* (1700). And yet there is no clear-cut proof that Masanobu belonged to any particular school. Although he had obviously studied the figure work of the first major designer of ukiyo-e prints, Hishikawa Moronobu, as well as that of the Torii masters Kiyonobu and Kiyomasu, he was apparently a self-taught artist.

Between 1703 and 1711, Masanobu designed the monochrome illustrations for at least twenty-two novels (*ukiyo-zōshi*) and puppet theater librettos (*rokudan-bon*). An examination of these books generally confirms his dependence on Hishikawa and Torii art,[30] and like all the popular novels of this period, their themes abound in literary allusions, fanciful historical episodes, and erotica.

Masanobu sometimes contributed to both the illustrations and the text of these publications. Indeed, his fondness for poetry and literature and his achievements as a writer are facts that cannot be ignored in any complete survey of his oeuvre. One of his literary feats, a modern version of the eleventh-century *Tale of Genji* in a series of three illustrated novels totaling eighteen volumes, was done while he was still in his early twenties. Admittedly, these books, the *Wakakusa Genji monogatari* (6 vols., 1707), the *Hinazuru Genji monogatari* (6 vols., 1708), and the *Kōhaku Genji monogatari* (6 vols., 1709), have a value that is perhaps more literary than pictorial. His prose was probably more stimulating to the Edo public than his illustrations (fig. 2), and it is hard to imagine, on the basis of these early designs, that Masanobu was destined to become one of the most influential ukiyo-e artists. After 1711 Masanobu illustrated very few books and his

---

*Superior numbers refer to bibliographical entries on page 48.

§The oldest and most important source of information on ukiyo-e artists is *Ukiyo-e ruikō*, compiled by Shokusanjin (Ōta Nampo) around 1790. Revised by Sasaya Kuninori in 1800. Subsequent version with additions entitled *Ukiyo-e ruikō tsuikō* by the novelist Santō Kyōden (Kitao Masanobu) in 1802. Revised by the writer Shikitei Samba around 1820. Further augmented in 1833 by the artist Keisai Eisen in *Mumeiō zuihitsu*. Revised with supplement and retitled *Zōho ukiyo-e ruikō* by Saitō Gesshin in 1844.

+Miyatake Gaikotsu[29] points out that Kammyō should be corrected to Shimmyō.

artistic efforts were apparently concentrated on the production of albums and large prints. Masanobu's early illustrated books give us the impression that he is in quest of his own style. And though we can perceive the awakening of a personal manner in the graceful delineation of the women in these works, his brushwork is too imitative to satisfy us completely.

Similarly, a study of Masanobu's early theatrical black-and-white prints (sumizuri-e) reveals his reliance on the Toriis. His greatest actor and Kabuki prints will be produced much later—in the early 1740s—when he reached the zenith of his artistic career with a fully matured style. The dominance of the Torii school in the field of theatrical prints and posters during Genroku was overwhelming. The forceful brush-line of Kiyonobu and Kiyomasu, featuring such mannerisms as "gourd-shaped legs" (hyōtan ashi) and "earth-worm lines" (mimizu-gaki), was no doubt well suited to the histrionics of the Kabuki, especially for violent (aragoto) scenes (fig. 18). On the other hand, the designs of beautiful women and actors in female roles (onnagata; there are no actresses in Kabuki) were stylistically in the direct lineage of Moronobu.

It would have been impossible for Masanobu to add more bombast to the brush-line of the reigning Toriis. He had to find a new path, create another mood, while absorbing the concepts of his rivals and making them his own. This he did in a way that was to reveal his genius and make him the unsurpassed master of the comic album.

THE COMIC ALBUMS

Starting from the Hōei era (1704–11) but mostly during the Shōtoku era (1711–16), Masanobu designed about twenty black-and-white albums, each usually containing twelve horizontal prints on a given theme—theatrical, literary, comic, erotic, or other. Each sheet, often numbered but unsigned except for the last one of the series, is in ōban size (about 26 by 38 cm.). These prints were sold either in folding albums (which would explain the center crease in many of the surviving sheets) or, it may be conjectured, individually as single sheets (ichimai-e) or even mounted as lateral scrolls (makimono) if the theme lent itself to this format. To date, the only attempt to catalogue these prints has been made by Professor Shibui,[47] the well-known ukiyo-e scholar and connoisseur.

One of Masanobu's greatest merits was to introduce humor in his themes. To be sure, this humor is never aimed at the ruling class. Nor does it try to ridicule or defend the little man by exploiting the grotesque or pathetic side of the urban scene. Being a native of the shogun's capital of Edo, Masanobu obviously knew the difference between amusing satire and hostile criticism, between gentle irreverence and insolent contempt. If people were to smile or laugh at the targets of his brush, the subjects had to be harmless or open to socially acceptable derision, for any violation of the Tokugawa ethical system, any sign of disrespect toward the regime, would have resulted in swift and severe punishment. The circumstances leading to Hanabusa Itchō's exile of sixteen years on Miyakejima—he was accused of lese majesty for painting a travesty of the boating excursions that Shogun Tsunayoshi made with his favorite mistress—clearly show that satire with political overtones was a luxury the town painter (machi eshi) could not afford.

If we give Masanobu credit for designing ukiyo-e's earliest comic prints, we should also remark that he frequently drew his inspiration from traditional themes and literary clichés of a legendary or classic past which are at the source of many ancient Japanese works of art. Of minor influence on Masanobu's comic prints are the Toba-e, so named after the delicious genre cartoons attributed to the artist-monk Toba Sōjō (1053–1114); these masterpieces of native wit seem to have gained a renewed popularity during Genroku, although we find in Masanobu's body of works but one specimen derived from this peculiar style (fig. 7).

Hanabusa Itchō (1652–1724), a Kanō-trained artist who painted many genre scenes, had perhaps more influence on Masanobu's comic oeuvre than has been usually conceded. This dandy of the Yoshiwara pleasure quarter, while he did not design prints, excelled in painting caricatures. The common man is gaily, if not humorously, portrayed, and Itchō's brush captures the verities of Edo life without a hint of bitterness, but rather with a lighthearted touch. He also interprets in his manner the traditional themes of China and Japan, and even though he rarely used the courtesan as a motif—a frequent subject in Masanobu's comic prints—we can observe that a kindred sense of fun enlivens the productions of both artists. On the whole, however, the range of Itchō's satire is broader than that of Masanobu's.

Masanobu's humor is of course more characteristic of ukiyo-e. He creates amusing situations out of dramatic scenes taken from Noh, jōruri (puppet dramas), or Kabuki plays. He also pokes fun at the

venerable and jovial seven gods of happiness, at mythical heroes and Zen patriarchs, and even at himself (figs. 4, 5). He parodies the classic novel Tale of Genji as well as Chinese and Japanese legends. He is adept at the use of paradox and antithesis, contrasting hedonistic beauties and ascetic "beasts," mixing reality and fiction, the sacred and the profane.

Some of his works were created on the occasion of the New Year and thus mirror the joyful spirit of the plebeian class during the festive season. A facetious subject (fig. 8) depicts Daikoku, one of the seven gods of happiness, opening up his enormous bag of riches only to reveal playful rats mimicking sumō wrestlers with Ebisu, another of the gods, acting as a referee. This is perhaps one of the earliest sumō prints on record. Another design (fig. 9) shows Ebisu riding astride a giant tai (red sea-bream) which he has caught with rod and line; five enthusiastic youths, dressed and coifed like him, are dancing merrily in the shallow surf around the auspicious fish.

To the untrained eye, Masanobu's prints may seem to contain too many allusions to an unfamiliar cultural past. But in fact these references seldom hinder his comic message. The antics of Kimpira (fig. 10), the joie de vivre of Hotei (fig. 11), the escapades of Bodhi Dharma (fig. 12), and the distractions of Priest Saigyō (fig. 13) are presented so straightforwardly that they require little explanation. It is as if Masanobu the philosopher is reminding his disciples that behind the solemn and often hypocritical facade of myth, religion, and human endeavors, there is always a back-door escape—that, after all, life is here to be enjoyed in this floating, fleeting world.

No doubt the format most congenial to Masanobu's artistic temperament was the kakemono-e (a print size measuring about 56 by 30 cm.). Figure 8 (a vertical print) and figure 9 (a horizontal print) are humorous examples that were presented in this format. In these large sheets, Masanobu could give full expression to his genius, particularly in depictions of beautiful women. Needless to say, the social and economic climate of the Genroku epoch as well as feminine fashions prevailing at the time had a profound influence on his interpretation of feminine beauty.

FEMININE PORTRAITURE

Though we trace the antecedents of feminine portraiture in ukiyo-e to the genre paintings produced by the town painters from the end of the fifteenth century to the beginning of the Edo period, and though there existed an unbroken line of graphic traditions from the inception of the indigenous manner of painting known as Yamato-e—in the style of the brushwork, in the treatment of colors, and in the choice of subjects—the courtesans designed by Masanobu and his contemporaries of the ukiyo-e school differ in many respects from the low-class women, such as itinerant prostitutes and bath attendants, painted by the early town painters.

Whereas the women in the genre paintings are shown unabashedly as they are—young, old, lovely or wretched, without any glamor—Masanobu's courtesans reflect, body and soul, the ideals of feminine beauty prevalent in Edo. Gone is the down-to-earth realism of the early genre style which gave us an accurate vision of the passing scene. We now step into a world of make-believe, where all the ladies, in sumptuous garb and stylish coiffure, are tall, refined, and elegant.

The French historian H. Taine, a contemporary of Baudelaire, observed quite perceptively that "each century, with its own circumstances, begets feelings and works of beauty of its own; and as the human race progresses, it leaves behind forms of society and types of perfection that are no more." Considering the circumstances under which the Edo merchants were permitted to create their own institutions and culture, the idolization and idealization of the courtesan in ukiyo-e were perhaps the corollary of their escapist materialism. Indeed, the courtesan was for them the symbol of feminine beauty, the paragon of esoteric accomplishments, and the arbiter of fashion.

The splendor of the kimono designs and the richness of their tie-dyed or painted colors deserve particular attention because, from Genroku on, the process of weaving, dyeing, and embroidering silk was transformed from an ordinary craft into a consummate art which reached its peak of development during the Bunka (1804–18) and Bunsei (1818–30) eras.[12] Consequently, the beautiful woman is closely associated with her attire, and fashion is conceived as an integral part of her femininity.

The question naturally arises as to why these courtesans' portraits leave an everlasting mark on Japanese art. The answer lies in the fact that Masanobu—to paraphrase Baudelaire who had Constantin Guys in mind when he made the remark more than a century ago—"was able to extract from the fashions of the day their poetic content; to elicit the eternal from the ephemeral." Certainly, the years 1710 to

1716 mark the culmination of Masanobu's efforts toward an idealization of feminine beauty. His ability to express the ideals of Genroku womanhood may owe something to the example of the Kaigetsudō and Torii masters (fig. 19). But what strikes us most is his immense talent to infuse warmth and charm into his models. His beautiful woman has human qualities that seem to make her less distant, if not less haughty, than the Kaigetsudō goddess of the demimonde.

Masanobu's courtesans usually appear in a conventional standing or seated posture. These full-length portraits in *kakemono-e* size are for the most part in black and white, with red lead (*tan*) occasionally added by hand. As evidenced in plates 1–4, Masanobu is in complete control of his brush: his lines have an assurance, individuality, and delicacy which will help him attain even greater stature and fame.

The print reproduced as plate 1 and other related designs have been the subject of a valuable monograph by Robert T. Paine,[41] who proved convincingly that this *kakemono-e* print should be dated prior to 1718 because a later date is ruled out by the financial retrenchment policy of Yoshimune, the eighth shogun, who banned prints of large dimensions. Furthermore, this print served as the prototype for the *hosoban* triptych designs of the three courtesans produced as lacquer prints between 1717 and the 1740s by all the major ukiyo-e artists.

There is something different in the pose of the Edo beauty in this print, at the top center of the pyramidal design: the hand which holds the smoking pipe is concealed within her sleeve. This distinctive pose, which will be repeated time after time, usually in the right-hand sheet of the *hosoban* triptychs (each sheet measuring about 30 by 15.5 cm.) depicting the three beauties, adds a coquettish touch to the design and is, of course, pure Masanobu. The Kyoto beauty, at the right, whose hand is lifting the lower part of her kimono and thereby exposing her feet, has a stereotyped pose. The Osaka beauty, at the left, is clad in kimono with long trailing sleeves, a typical attire for the fashionable women of the city.

Masanobu's theme of the courtesans of the three cities, along with the pose of the Edo beauty, eventually proved so appealing that they formed a tradition. The countless imitations and derivations thereof tangibly demonstrate Masanobu's creative genius and preeminence in the ukiyo-e world during the first half of the eighteenth century.

In view of the paucity of reliable historical facts pertaining to the beginnings of ukiyo-e prints and the fairly limited number of known designs, it is hard to gauge the contemporary popularity of the early ukiyo-e depictions of beautiful women. Undoubtedly, these prints served as fashion plates, as pin-ups, or as souvenirs; but they were, as well, marvelous portraits of the nightless city's leading queens.

The surviving courtesan prints in the *kakemono-e* size of this golden age are not only extremely rare—perhaps even rarer than Sharaku's works—but are often considered to be among the most treasured possessions of ukiyo-e collectors.

MASANOBU THE PUBLISHER: THE KYŌHŌ ERA

SOCIAL CONDITIONS

The "happy society" of the Genroku epoch could not last forever. The extravagance of the ruling class, particularly during Shogun Tsunayoshi's reign (1680–1709), fiscal mismanagement, and the high cost of bringing relief to disaster areas had considerably weakened the treasury of the shogunate.

At the beginning of the Kyōhō era (1716–36), it fell upon Shogun Yoshimune to initiate a policy of retrenchment, the dual aim of which was to extricate the shogunate from its financial embarrassment and to put restraints on the affluent bourgeoisie. Based on frugality and feudal simplicity, this policy showed at first some signs of success; however, the reforms were bound to fail because the rice-oriented economic system of the Tokugawa regime could no longer cope with the financial needs of the privileged class. Consequently, the samurai fell further into debt, and the merchants continued to prosper.

Of course, tradesmen toed the official line and avoided overt displays of wealth. But plebeian culture retained its gaudy characteristics and pervasive influence. Despite the fact that warriors were admonished to eat and drink moderately and shun sensual pleasures, the primal cause of human vicissitude according to Confucianists, "the samurai and even the daimyō," in the words of Sansom,[42] "were taking to vulgar pastimes, visiting the theatres, composing irregular verses and singing popular songs. Their wives, old-fashioned people said, were better acquainted with the names and ages of popular actors than with the use of the needle."

Among all the amusements townspeople could easily afford, none attained the popularity of the Kabuki. No wonder then that during the 1720s and 1730s actors became the favorite subject matter of

ukiyo-e, such designs outnumbering those of courtesans or any other subject matter. Because of the retrenchment policy, ukiyo-e publishers abstained from issuing prints in *kakemono-e* size soon after 1718 and sold most of their production in the much smaller *hosoban* size (about 30 by 15.5 cm.) with full coloring added by hand. Technically, these designs were usually printed on sheets measuring about 30 by 47 cm., which were then cut into three prints: hence the proliferation of *hosoban* triptychs, of which a few specimens have survived uncut.

Apart from political considerations, commercial benefit may have been the reason why publishers turned to these small narrow sheets: their size and subject matter were made to appeal to a wider segment of the buying public; they could be printed and hand-colored swiftly and cheaply; they could be easily peddled, and they sold well. The rise in the number of wholesale publishers in Edo during the Kyōhō era—from four in the 1680s to thirty in 1730—proves that the demand for illustrated books and prints was quite high.

There is ample evidence that the totality of Masanobu's work done until 1718 was published by well-known publishers, principally Ya-maguchi-ya, Kiku-ya, Nishimura-ya, Komatsu-ya, and Iga-ya. It seems likely that Masanobu opened his own wholesale publishing shop by the name of Okumura-ya in Tōri Shio-chō around 1721 when he started using a red gourd-shaped sign as his trademark. Indeed, during the 1720s and 1730s he often advertised his status as an *ezōshi toiya* or *ezōshi oroshi* (wholesaler of illustrated books), together with other claims, in rectangular panels placed at the bottom of his prints. It was probably not until 1734 that he took the studio name of Hōgetsudō and the art name Tanchōsai. And subsequent to the adoption of these new names, it appears that the previous pseudonym Shimmyō fell into disuse. In all likelihood, the Edo *haiku* master Shōgetsudō Fukaku Sen-ō (1662–1753) bestowed upon Masanobu the pseudonyms Hōgetsudō and Bunkaku. On the other hand, "Baiō," the author of the illustrated novel *Wakakusa Genji monogatari* (1707), and "Baigin," the author of *Fūryū kagami ga ike* (1709), were most certainly *noms de plume* adopted by Masanobu.

THE LACQUER PRINT

At this juncture, a few words on the development of ukiyo-e techniques may be of interest to the reader. In point of time, hand-colored prints were produced during the Genroku era (1688–1704). It was reported that in Hōei (1704–11) and Shōtoku (1711–16), black-and-white prints were occasionally hand-colored with red lead (*tan*; see pls. 1–4). Other colors, particularly a dark-red dye extracted from sapanwood (*sibō*), yellow (obtained from gamboge), lilac, brown, and blue, were also used. To this limited palette, *beni* (a rose-red dye derived from safflower) was added as a dominant color around 1716 to produce so-called *beni-e*. Santō Kyōden, in the *Ukiyo-e ruikō tsuikō*, attributed the invention of *beni-e* to the publisher Izumi-ya Gonshirō of Asakusa Mitsuke, Dōbō-chō. Improvements were made by hand-applying black ink with which glue had been mixed to obtain a glossy finish and by occasionally sprinkling brass powder over the "lacquer" for decorative effect. Such prints (see pls. 5–15) came to be called "lacquer prints" (*urushi-e*), although in Masanobu's time the generic term of *beni-e* was commonly applied to *urushi-e*.

It is possible that the lacquering technique was invented by Masanobu, though there appears to be no documentary proof to support this fact. Masanobu's claim that he was "the originator of one school of ukiyo-e, without equal" (*ukiyo-e ichi-ryū kongen, rui nashi*) was no doubt a boast that bore no relevance to the creation of *urushi-e* technique; it probably referred to his personal manner as opposed to the Torii style prevailing in the field of theatrical programs, posters, and prints. An examination of the lacquer prints done by Masanobu prior to his establishment as a publisher is not conclusive: it merely suggests that he was one of the first artists to take full advantage of this new technique. The print reproduced as plate 7, depicting an actor playing the role of Oshichi—identified by the crest of Arashi Kiyosaburō (d. 1713), who first enacted that role—was published by Sōshū(Sagami)-ya, circa 1718. Yet at about the same time, and perhaps as early as 1717, several publishers were issuing lacquer prints designed by other artists. We would be inclined to surmise that the lacquer print, like the *beni-e*, was probably the invention of a publisher. As the leader of the "ukiyo-e quartet"[67] (publisher, designer, engraver, and printer), the publisher not only financed and coordinated the activities of these artists and artisans, but also assigned the important tasks of hand-coloring, lacquering, and the sprinkling of metal dust to skilled pieceworkers.

As we survey Masanobu's hand-colored works in *hosoban* size, we are faced with the difficulty of separating his designs of beautiful women (*bijin*) from those of Kabuki actors in female roles (*onnagata*). This difficulty is not so much a matter of identity as one of style since both types of "women" are graphically expressed with the same countenance and—omitting female warriors—feminine poses. Plate 5 is a typical example of this artistic ambivalence. This print portrays a female impersonator (iroko) whose kimono is decorated with the characters Ōsaka and the conspicuous crest of Sanokawa Mangiku, clear indications that the famous actor, like a courtesan of the three cities, personifies the city of Osaka. In the delineation of Mangiku, the artist has deliberately eschewed all signs of masculinity: the facial expression, the colorful kimono with long trailing sleeves, the mien of feigned timidity, all of these characterize depictions of beautiful women.

Thus for the sake of convenience and in order to appraise the artistic value of Masanobu's hosoban sheets, they will be divided into three groups: 1) Kabuki actor prints, excluding figures of actors in female roles (onnagata); 2) prints of courtesans and actors in female roles (onnagata); and 3) bird-and-flower (kachō) prints and other subjects.

PRINTS OF KABUKI ACTORS

At a time when Kiyonobu I and Kiyomasu I were relatively inactive or nearing retirement and all Kabuki expression was still keyed to their style, Masanobu came out with actor prints singularly free from Torii bombast, each one a gem of studied elegance. In fact, Masanobu's lacquer prints, together with those of his pupil Toshinobu[13] (fl. 1717–40s), constitute the most important body of work produced in this technique; they are outstanding in both number and quality. By comparison, the work of their chief rivals—among them Kondō Kiyoharu, Kiyomasu II, Kiyonobu II, Nishimura Shigenaga—appears somewhat meretricious, for they often lapsed into mediocre imitations of either the first Toriis or the Okumuras.

In the early 1720s Masanobu could truly proclaim, and without any immodesty, that he was "the originator of one school of ukiyo-e," that he was now "sans pareil." He reminds us of the self-centered Courbet, who called himself "the master-painter" and boasted in writing that "in everybody's opinion, I am the first man of France."

Plate 6 and figure 20, which depict, respectively, Ogino Isaburō and Ichikawa Monnosuke, and figure 21, depicting Ichimura Takenojō with Sanokawa Mangiku, are representative examples of Masanobu's actor prints. See to what extent his brushwork has been liberated from the confines of the Torii stereotype and to what degree the draftsmanship and the minute details of the compositions have become unmistakably his. Within the limits of the hosoban format, it is surprising how Masanobu has exploited to the fullest a combination of elegant brush-lines and brilliant colors, thereby compensating for the loss of the robust simplicity and black-and-white intensity that characterized the larger prints of Genroku.

In this context, plates 8 and 9, both portraying Ichikawa Danjūrō II, typify the profound changes that took place in Masanobu's rendering of Kabuki subjects; the former, depicting Danjūrō as a vegetable vendor and dating to 1726, has a dynamic quality which perhaps still hints at Kiyonobu, though by and large it clearly bears the mark of Masanobu's individual style; the latter, a portrait of the famous actor as Soga no Gorō and done seven years later, in 1733, shows virtually no trace of Torii influence. Both designs are striking hosoban specimens of the Kyōhō era.

The admirers of early black-and-white prints and tan-e (black-and-white prints with red lead or tan added by hand) are partly justified in pointing out that something has been irretrievably lost in this evolution, and that the delicacy of line and profusion of tone and glitter in the hand-colored lacquer prints will never replace the vigor of contours, the inherent grandeur of Genroku masterpieces. And while conceding this loss, Fenollosa, the doyen of ukiyo-e critics, remarked judiciously that "in the finer specimens [of lacquer prints] splendid harmonies were achieved.... These schemes of colouring were something absolutely new not only in Ukiyo-ye but in Japanese art. They were the experiments in colour which an independent popular consciousness was making, experiments destined profoundly to affect the future of all Japanese industries, and eventually the colour-sense of the world."[7]

Perhaps the hand-colored lacquer prints, more than benizuri-e (prints with two or three block-printed colors that appeared in the 1740s), heralded the advent of the nishiki-e or "brocade" prints, the full-color woodblock prints of Japan that enchanted and influenced the art of Whistler, Mary Cassatt, Van Gogh, Degas, and Toulouse-Lautrec.

COURTESAN AND ONNAGATA PRINTS

The qualities of Masanobu's brush-lines were eminently suited for the portrayal of Kabuki actors in female roles (onnagata; pls. 10 and 12) and the courtesan (pls. 11 and 13). His lacquer prints in hosoban

size have much charm and are of a high artistic level, although they leave us with the impression that he only applied on a smaller scale what he had already achieved so successfully with his superb kakemono-e designs of the mid 1710s.

Figure 22, reminiscent in its pyramidal composition of his early kakemono-e of the courtesans of the three cities (pl. 1), amuses us by its satire. The woman at the top center, with a garment over her head, is striking a Daruma-like pose; the roll of scripture (in this instance a map of the Yoshiwara licensed quarter) and the broom held by her attendants are allusions to Kanzan and Jittoku, the two Zen hermits. The print is signed as from "the genuine brush of Okumura Masanobu." And part of the inscription in the circular cartouche, at the bottom right, reads, "since my prints are being spuriously published I put on the mark of the gourd." Masanobu was apparently warning the public against works that were either faked or copied. Unfortunately, his attempts at exposing the frauds were in vain. As we have already remarked, the theme of the courtesans of the three cities, for example, was not only pirated by Masanobu's contemporaries, but with innumerable variations it formed a tradition that lasted until the middle of the eighteenth century.

As an interesting digression, it should be noted that at about the same time William Hogarth's work, in England, was much plagiarized. In his case, he petitioned the authorities and obtained a ruling in his favor with the Copyright Act of 1735. His series of etchings, Rake's Progress, were the first prints ever to bear the inscription "published according to Act of Parliament," a good protection for Hogarth and a warning to unscrupulous publishers and artists.

BIRD-AND-FLOWER PRINTS

Robert T. Paine,[40] whose studies on ukiyo-e artists, particularly Masanobu, deserve much praise, pointed out that one of the sources of Masanobu's bird-and-flower (kachō) designs and other subjects done in the Kanō style was a book entitled Wakan meihitsu ehon tekagami (literally, "Famous Brushes of Japan and China: The Hand-Mirror Picture Book"), published in 1720 and illustrated by Ōoka Shumboku.[27] There is no denying that the charming composition of plate 14, showing sparrows in the snow, was the result of juxtaposing two separate designs in Shumboku's book. His Cock on a Jar of Rice (fig. 23), as well as a hawk design and a portrait of Sugawara Michizane in Chinese robe, were also based on designs in the Ehon tekagami.

To be sure, Masanobu's versions of Shumboku's models, being hand-colored, add some luster to the rather bland book illustrations. His rendering of the sparrows gives us a heightened variation of the original; his cock perched on a jar is indeed pecking at rice grains, a clever improvement over the earlier Shumboku design. Yet some undefinable element is lacking in these bird-and-flower prints; it is as if they were inspired by an indifferent attitude toward nature. To the Japanese artist, "the aim of painting kachō-ga has, in the first place, never been simply to depict birds, flowers, and the like, but by depicting them to express some feeling about life."[32] Ingenious and gifted as he was, Masanobu failed to produce bird-and-flower masterpieces equal to those of Itō Jakuchū and Kanyōsai, who were entirely independent of the ukiyo-e school. He did only a few such prints in the mid 1720s and soon lost interest in this short-lived experiment. Perhaps Masanobu's business preoccupations, his dependence on the imitative, and his lack of creative conviction in dealing with subjects alien to the Kabuki and Yoshiwara prevented him from achieving a bird-and-flower oeuvre worthy of his name.

LANDSCAPES

The preceding remarks would also apply, for the most part, to his hosoban lacquer prints with landscape motifs, a specimen of which is shown in figure 24. It seems that this kind of print came in vogue at the end of the 1720s when three artists—Nishimura Shigenaga, Torii Kiyomasu II, and Masanobu—vied with each other in designing similar vertical series celebrating the "Eight Views of Lake Biwa" (Ōmi hakkei).*

---

*Shigenaga's Ōmi hakkei was published by Emi-ya, and in rapid succession Edo hakkei and Kanazawa hakkei, companion sets of eight prints each, were offered to the public; later, Shigenaga executed a vertical landscape series on the theme of Nana Komachi ("The Seven Komachi") as well as a set called Fūryū shiki no kōsaku ("Refined Four Seasons of Farming"). Not to be outdone, Kiyomasu II came out with his own version of Ōmi hakkei, published by Iga-ya, and other series entitled Nana Komachi, Shiki no hyakushō ("The Farmer's Four Seasons"), and Go sekku ("The Five Festivals"). To this surfeit of upright designs, we might add the following series in the hosoban horizontal format: Shin Yoshiwara hakkei ("Eight Views of New Yoshiwara") and Go sekku by Okumura Masanobu, Shiki no asobi ("The Amusements of the Four Seasons") by Okumura Toshinobu, Kamakura hakkei by Kondō Kiyoharu, Mu Tamagawa ("The Six Crystal Rivers") and Yoshiwara hakkei by Torii Kiyomasu II, Edo hakkei by Torii Kiyonobu II, and another Nana Komachi set by Shigenaga.

Although little is known about the development of these landscape designs, we should bear in mind that bird-and-flower and landscape prints, in the tradition of Kōrin and Kenzan, and principally under the influence of the Kanō academy, were produced by most of the ukiyo-e artists of the eighteenth century. Never as popular as actor and courtesan prints, their presence nonetheless confirmed the enduring and exoteric appeal of pictorial representations of nature among the common people. But had it not been for the masterpieces Hokusai and Hiroshige created in the 1830s, it is doubtful whether bird-and-flower and landscape prints would ever have taken their rightful place in the repertoire of ukiyo-e.

CHINESE SUBJECTS

Chinese lore and literature have often laid emphasis on tales of the marvelous and supernatural as well as those extolling the virtues of generosity, filial piety, and family loyalties. The contents of these legends and moralistic stories were borrowed extensively by Masanobu and his rivals. These borrowings took the appearance of thinly disguised parodies (see fig. 5) or underwent fanciful transformations —a much used ukiyo-e device called *mitate* (see figures 7, 17).

Now and then the graphic derivation remained essentially Chinese, unaltered by artistic license. Plate 15, for example, from a series devoted to "The Twenty-four Paragons of Filial Piety," is an illustration of the Confucian story of Kakkyo, the exemplary son. Too destitute to take proper care of his mother, Kakkyo, with his wife's consent, decided to dispose of their son so as to reduce the family burden. As he was digging a hole in the ground to bury the child, he struck a pot filled with gold. The son was saved, the house prospered, and they all lived happily ever after. Apart from its moral teaching, Masanobu's depiction of Kakkyo's miraculous find reveals a rather astigmatic Japanese view of Chinese peasants. Kakkyo looks more like a wealthy landlord of the Ch'ing dynasty than a poor farmer of the Middle Kingdom. Despite this inaccuracy, the feeling of gratitude shown by Kakkyo, the startled expression of his wife, and the quiet dignity of the couple lend subtle sensitivity to the composition.

STONE-RUBBING PRINTS

In the last days of Kyōhō (1716–36), or perhaps during the Gembun era (1736–41), Masanobu experimented with *ishizuri*, a technique named after Chinese monochrome stone rubbings which it tried to imitate. These "stone-rubbing" prints were actually printed from a woodblock on which the outlines were incised rather than engraved in relief, and therefore did not receive any black ink. They featured a black background with contrasting white lines. However, a close scrutiny of Masanobu's *ishizuri-e* reveals that the engraver had recourse to a mixed "reserve and relief" method, a type of carving that Azechi, the noted modern print artist, calls "negative and positive."[2] Figure 25, which portrays two legendary Chinese sages, clearly shows that the outlines of Kanyu's head and arms, his companion's facial features, and the ox and other minor parts of the design were engraved in relief. In a stone rubbing the sages' faces and the ox would normally appear in black with their outlines reserved in white. Thus the skillful use of *ishizuri* allowed contrasts of line and space that the ancient Chinese medium rarely achieved.

In truth, it seems pointless to discuss the respective merits of the Chinese and Japanese techniques because stone rubbings existed in China only as an adjunct to art. Unlike Japanese prints, they were not an end in themselves, but were considered merely as representations of famous stone carvings; unlike Japanese prints, they were not meant to have mass appeal, but served as reference material for an elite of mandarin-scholars.

Masanobu produced only a few *ishizuri-e* in *hosoban* size and confined his themes mainly to Chinese legends and the *Tale of Genji*. Once the stir created by the newness—or rather the revitalization —of this medium wore off, he probably realized that little was to be gained from espousing a reproductive technique whose contribution to the art of ukiyo-e was bound to be very limited.

EROTICA

No study of Masanobu's work would be complete without mention of his erotic oeuvre. Like all of the major ukiyo-e artists—excepting perhaps Sharaku—Masanobu produced *shunga* (literally, "spring pictures") in albums, illustrated books, and paintings. His erotic illustrated books and series of broadsheets were catalogued in 1926–28 by Professor Shibui in the most important and comprehensive survey to date on the subject of early *shunga*.[46]

A glance at the corpus of Masanobu's surviving erotica should suffice to convince anyone that it is quite large, the largest part accounted for by his illustrated erotic books (*kōshoku-bon* and *enshoku-*

bon). His best *shunga* designs, however, are horizontal *ōban* black-and-white prints with occasional hand-coloring.

Artistically, Masanobu's erotica is uneven: it fluctuates between the uninspired and the highly creative, the frankly pornographic and the near sublime. During the Genroku epoch (1688–1716), his *ōban* and *chūban* (about 20 by 30 cm.) compositions often lacked the originality and skill of his illustrious predecessors in the *genre galant*, Hishikawa Moronobu and Sugimura Jihei. In this early period, Masanobu's nudes or seminudes and his depictions of the physical act are frequently awkward and denote an imperfect mastery of human anatomy. But Masanobu, a self-taught artist, had great capacity for learning from other masters. Gradually, and perhaps under the influence of Nishikawa Sukenobu (1671–1750),[63] the Kyoto artist (fig. 27), Masanobu's brushwork turned to a softer and more intimate manner until at last, in the 1730s, his lines acquired that delicacy so characteristic of his depictions of beautiful women.

Plate 16, a well-known design from a series entitled *Some-iro no yama, neya no hinagata* ("Mountain of Dyed Color, Examples of Bedrooms"), was published in the mid 1730s. The cover sheet from an album of twelve hand-colored *ōban* black-and-white prints, this print, done in a restrained manner, is representative of Masanobu's best and certainly most mature erotic work. Its splendid composition and exquisite hand-coloring have always elicited much envy and admiration. So much so that the late Louis V. Ledoux,[21] whose discriminating taste in ukiyo-e has seldom been equaled, included this design in his collection, which contained only four *shunga* prints (exclusively cover sheets of the "primitive" period) out of a total of 258 items. The fact that this design met the exacting aesthetic standards set by Ledoux for his collection is testimony to Masanobu's artistic genius.

MASANOBU UNRIVALED: THE 1740s

We now enter into the most brilliant decade of Masanobu's artistic career. The 1740s witnessed the full ripening of his genius, the birth of the perspective print, the invention of the pillar print, and the advent of the two-color print. During this period, Masanobu produced nearly a score of hand-colored prints depicting beautiful women and Kabuki actors in *kakemono-e* size that are generally regarded as the ultimate achievement of the "primitive" period. "In line composition," according to Fenollosa,[6] these figures are "the finest proportioned, the most solid, the firmest in pose, the most soberly complete in designing." Of these masterpieces we shall have more to say later.

Chronologically, the decade began at the close of the Gembun era (1736–41), extended through the Kampō (1741–44) and the Enkyō (1744–48) eras, and ended in the middle of the Kan'en era (1748–51). The politico-social structure of the country remained unchanged, even after the abdication in 1745 of Yoshimune, the able eighth shogun, in favor of his first-born son, the incompetent and debauched Ieshige (ruled 1745–60).

It may be appropriate to say a few words about the impact of Dutch civilization on the Japanese since the principle of European perspective was most probably introduced in Japan by the Hollanders.[56] Contrary to a widely accepted belief, Shogun Yoshimune's sumptuary and repressive edicts of Kyōhō—which upheld Iemitsu's (ruled 1623–51) longstanding ban on works connected with Christianity—did not specifically proscribe the study of the Dutch language or the import of Dutch books. But only the few *Rangakusha* (literally, "Holland scholars") and official interpreters at Deshima were allowed to communicate with the "red-haired barbarians" and master the complexities of Western sciences such as cartography, geography, botany, medicine, and astronomy. It followed that these studies, like a forbidden fruit, had aroused the curiosity of those who were denied access to the knowledge of the Hollanders. Paralleling this interest in the culture, sciences, and arts of the Occident was a relaxation of the ban on large prints.

PERSPECTIVE PRINTS

Thus at the end of 1740 Masanobu, always in the forefront of artistic innovation, produced some extraordinary prints, sensational in format and novel in concept. Ranging in size from about 33 by 46 cm. to about 46 by 68 cm., these very large *ōban* and extra-large *ōban* horizontal prints featured a linear perspective, a device hitherto unused in Japanese art. It was perhaps inevitable that Masanobu, after his first peep at Dutch copperplate engravings, would experiment with European perspective and integrate it into ukiyo-e. His efforts were crowned with success, although it seems open to question whether the *uki-e* (literally, "floating pictures") really appealed to the Edo masses, long familiar with the optical distortions of conventional isometry. Perhaps the concept of the vanishing point was to them what the principle of simultaneity, as developed by Picasso, is now to us: an expression of artistic audacity and a proof that new graphic devices are rarely subordinated to the laws of nature.

Masanobu's perspective prints are all the more interesting because of his ability to create scenes characteristic of Edo life, filled with gregarious townspeople in spirited action. He shows great resource in the handling of urban crowds. Whether the multitude consists of Kabuki enthusiasts (pl. 20), or teahouse hedonists (pls. 17, 18), or habitués of the Yoshiwara gay quarter in pursuit of lucre or love (pl. 19), all of the figures are so meticulously delineated and the surroundings so precisely drawn that they give the social historian an accurate view of the "floating world."

Plate 20, which depicts the interior of the Nakamura-za Kabuki theater, is considered one of Masanobu's perspective masterpieces. This print attests to his amazing powers of observation and shows how effectively he could re-create the atmosphere of a Kabuki theater. Each part of the design is skillfully organized: animated spectators, some eating and some drinking while enjoying the play, fill the foreground; the stage, with Ichikawa Ebizō in the role of Yanone Gorō, is the focus of the central part of the print; the upper half is dominated by the geometric patterns of the ceiling, pillars, and large paper lanterns. Nowhere is there a superfluous detail, and the static, melodramatic pose of the actor constitutes an admirable counterpoise to the liveliness of the theatergoers. To a great extent the unity of this composition is achieved through linear perspective.

When Masanobu took some liberties with the new European device, as in the case of plate 17, where parallel lines diverge in several directions from the center of the sheet, the effect of perspective is obviously negated by the graphic parallelism. And yet this particular print has a redeeming feature: on the second floor of the teahouse, persons in merriment are seen through the translucency of the sliding partitions. These black silhouettes—more akin to a galanty show than a precise rendering of shadow—add a very original note to the design.

Plates 18 and 19 display Masanobu's clever blending of celebrated Edo landscapes with the rectilinearity of European perspective. We are able to catch a glimpse of the Sumida River near the Ryōgoku Bridge (pl. 18), and the *Gojikken-michi*—the final section of the *Nihon-zutsumi* (the Japan Dike)—which led to the precincts of Edo's principal gay quarter, the Yoshiwara (pl. 19). Minor in scale as they are, these landscapes contribute in no small way to the harmony of the compositions.

It will not escape the viewer of Masanobu's perspective prints, especially the extra-large broadsheets (e.g., pl. 20), that their publisher was Genroku of the Okumura-ya. Although the traditional biographies of ukiyo-e artists (see footnote on page 33) tell us that both Genroku and Gempachi were Masanobu's personal names, the truth, based on circumstantial evidence, is that they could not have belonged to one and the same person. Okumura Genroku was probably an adopted son of Masanobu, and his career as an artist and publisher has been partially reconstructed.[64] Late in the 1730s Masanobu transferred the management of his wholesale publishing house to Genroku, so as to free himself from business commitments and devote more time to his art.

It goes without saying that perspective prints, from the outset, were imitated by Masanobu's contemporaries, among them Nishimura Shigenaga, Furuyama Moromasa, Torii Kiyotada, Tanaka Masunobu, Jōgetsudō, and Kōgetsudō. Each is known to have produced one or more of these *uki-e*, but there seems to be no remarkable strength and no great merit in their work.

PILLAR PRINTS

Much has been written about various types of elongated prints called "pillar pictures" (*hashira-e*), so named because their shape was well fitted for the purpose of decorating the supporting pillars—as well as other parts of the interior—of plebeian homes. The word *hashira-e* was most likely coined by Masanobu, and his claim to the invention of the pillar print has been generally recognized. For no other artist has professed to be "the originator of pillar prints" (*hashira-e kongen*). It should be noted, however, that the earliest *hashira-e* design and the date when it first appeared are unknown.

It seems that Masanobu applied the generic term of *hashira-e* to several types of prints, of varying heights and widths, which for clarity's sake are described as follows:

Type	Approx. measurements	Classification	Example
A	127 × 15.5 cm.	extra-tall *hashira-e*	plate 21
B	71 × 15.5 cm.	*hashira-e*	plate 25
C	71 × 12 cm.	narrow *hashira-e*	figure 28
D	66 × 25 cm.	*kakemono-e*	plate 26

Pillar prints of types A, B, and C came with a width (not exceeding 15.5 cm.) which one may regard as *sui generis*, whereas the widest type (type D), also called *kakemono-e* in Masanobu's time, had a width of about 25 cm. Although taller (by about 10 cm.) and narrower (by about 5 cm.) than the *kakemono-e* prints of the Genroku epoch, we deem it preferable and perhaps more appropriate to treat prints of type D not as pillar prints but as *kakemono-e* prints, in a category where they really belong.

One of the first pillar prints probably made its appearance in 1741 (the year Sanokawa Ichimatsu I came to Edo), and quite possibly the spectacular size was due to Masanobu's propensity to amaze his public. Of the extra-tall *hashira-e* only three prints are extant, of which plate 21 reproduces one, a superb portrait of Ichimatsu.

Because of its peculiar format, the creation of a pillar print must have been no easy task. Frank Lloyd Wright, the architect who was commissioned by the Spaulding brothers to purchase part of their extensive ukiyo-e collection (now in the Museum of Fine Arts, Boston), once remarked that the *hashira-e* was "the most decorative and difficult form of Japanese print." Just as, to a Chinese carver, the curvature of an ivory tusk taxed his ingenuity, so in a similar way the tall and narrow confines of the pillar print presented a challenge to Masanobu's artistry.

The composition of the pillar print depended upon a dual exigency, which was to bring into prominence the essential part of the design, and, of necessity, to eliminate every inessential or secondary element that might detract from its uniqueness of form and content. Masanobu knew full well that some sort of artistic "surgery" was fundamental to the design of the pillar print. The following example will demonstrate Masanobu's shrewdness and his ability to transform, without apparent effort, a good print of *kakemono-e* size into a successful pillar print. Plate 22, a pillar print showing the standing figure of a courtesan (*oiran*) and her young female attendant (*kamuro*), was pulled from a woodblock identical to that of a wider version in *kakemono-e* size (pl. 23). A close examination of the latter print reveals a vertical break that runs from shoulder to heel on the standing figure. The presence of this unusual flaw has given rise to the speculation that the *kakemono-e* design was created by adapting a second woodblock to the earlier pillar print block. However, the survival of a "first" impression of the same *kakemono-e* design (pl. 24), unmarred by any vertical break, has very much weakened the credibility of this conjecture.

Apart from pillar prints resulting from a clever trimming of *kakemono-e* designs, Masanobu conceived, within the confines of this demanding format, works of great originality. In fact the pillar print proved an ideal vehicle for Masanobu's creative powers. The realistic portrait (pl. 25) of Fukai Shidōken (1682–1765)—notorious for his quasi-Rabelaisian jests which he emphasized with a wooden phallic symbol—conveys well the lecherous nature and physical ugliness of this inimitable and immensely popular raconteur. The depiction of Shōki with a straw hat (fig. 28) is a masterly example of ingenious pillar print design and dramatic composition. It is bold, uncluttered, kinetic, and strong enough to suggest the impending doom of evil spirits. Shōki is ready to quell the demons with his ferocious look and modish straw hat! This refreshing variation on a hackneyed Chinese theme displays that same sense of humor so typical of Masanobu's early comic prints.

KAKEMONO-E MASTERPIECES

However, it is on prints of *kakemono-e* size that Masanobu, now sure of himself, will expend his major effort, where the delicacy of his lines will reach a point of perfection seldom equaled by other ukiyo-e masters.

Plate 26, a portrait of the actor Onoe Kikugorō I, has been described by Noguchi Yonejirō as "easily one of the greatest works of Masanobu,"[37] while plate 27, another portrait of the same actor, has been hailed by Professor Narazaki as "a masterpiece, not only among the works of Masanobu, but in all ukiyo-e."[31]

We marvel at the skill of Masanobu's brushwork and his remarkable gift to impart a feeling of lifelike naturalness to his subject. In both examples, the handsome and sensuous features of Kikugorō, the exquisite pattern of his kimono enhanced by brilliant handcoloring, the ideal placement of the poem and signature, the mastery of the execution, and mainly the magnificence of a fully matured personal style, all combine to make these portraits the most prized and sought-after prints in ukiyo-e. Indeed, these two *kakemono-e* of superlative distinction and exceptional beauty are the expression *par excellence* of the Japanese genius, and they are worthy to be ranked among the world's masterpieces of graphic art.

By no means are such felicitous creations unique among the *kakemono-e* prints produced by Masanobu during the 1740s. Several other works of capital importance have fortunately survived. The print reproduced in plate 28 depicts a young woman caught in a gust of wind, capturing her in a pose of sensual charm that is instinctively feminine and altogether delightful. Some thirty-five years later (ca. 1780), Torii Kiyonaga, on a narrow pillar print, will exploit the same theme, perhaps with more voluptuousness and ornamentation, but without the flavor of the Masanobu original.

The print showing a courtesan whispering instructions to her attendant in a tender embrace (fig. 29), or that of the actor Ichikawa Ebizō in the swashbuckling role of Sukeroku (fig. 30), have a purity of line and an emotional content that compel our admiration. Print after print, the idols of the Edo masses remain Masanobu's persistent motif, the *raison d'être* of his prolific output. "Inspiration is having only one thing to say and never being tired of saying it," remarked the critic Jean Paulhan of "N.R.F." (*Nouvelle Revue Française*) fame. It is quite apparent that the cogency of this definition has particular relevance to the floating world of Okumura Masanobu.

Now in his late fifties, Masanobu finally reached the peak of his art. Not only was he the undisputed leader of the ukiyo-e school, a position he had held for over two decades, but he also eclipsed all his rivals, old and new. Indeed, a survey of the prints issued during the Kampō (1741–44) and Enkyō (1744–48) eras by the Toriis of the second generation, Furuyama Moromasa, Nishimura Shigenaga, and other artists of the second rank—with the possible exception of Ishikawa Toyonobu—reveals their indebtedness to Masanobu's style as well as a certain superficiality in their work.

ILLUSTRATED BOOKS

Although much space has been allotted to an examination of Masanobu's prints, since they undoubtedly constitute the most significant part of his work, still another aspect of his oeuvre, namely his book illustrations, cannot be passed over in complete silence. Whatever their artistic worth, illustrated books were probably, from a business point of view, the mainstay of the Okumura-ya publishing house. Throughout his long career, Masanobu produced an impressive quantity of designs for a very large number of novels (*ukiyo-zōshi*), puppet theater librettos (*rokudan-bon*), erotic books (*enshoku-bon*), and "picture books" (*ehon*).

It cannot be said that the development of Masanobu's book illustrations followed the same path as that of his broadsheets. Generally speaking, in fact, there is little to suggest, in the illustrations of Masanobu's books issued during the Genroku epoch, that they were made by an innovative and talented artist. The merit of these early publications, if any, lay more in their literary content than in their designs, which were few. For example, the six volumes of the *Wakakusa Genji monogatari* (1707) contained only twenty-nine designs, or an average of five designs per volume (only four in volume one).

Some measure of artistic success was achieved toward the end of the 1730s, but mostly in the 1740s and 1750s, with the issuance of a different type of book in which the text was always ancillary to the illustrations. As implied by their epithet *ehon*, these publications were primarily picture books and contained an illustration on virtually every page. Depending on their theme, they featured images of the passing urban scene or of a cultural past rich in legends, traditions, and erotica.

The designs for Masanobu's "picture books" show a marked improvement over those of his early illustrated novels. Yet on the whole they seem to lack the graphic elements that made Masanobu the leading artist of his time. Quite probably, many of these illustrations were made by junior artists or apprentice-followers working in his studio, and this may account for the uneven quality of the designs. In some instances (as in the case of the *Ehon Ogura nishiki*), it appears that Masanobu attached greater importance to the poems or commentaries accompanying the illustrations than to the illustrations themselves. In other instances (as in the case of the *Ehon Edo-e sudare byōbu*, where most of the text is replaced by short captions), we have the impression that the designs were done in haste, that he relied too much on the facility of his brush and too little on his own inspiration.

Among the many picture books published by Masanobu, the following titles should be mentioned: *Ehon Kinryūzan Asakusa sembonzakura* (two volumes, 1734), *Ehon Ogura nishiki* (five volumes, 1740), *Ehon Edo-e sudare byōbu* (two volumes), *Ehon musha Edo-murasaki susokon* (two volumes), *Ehon tsuru no hashi* (two volumes, 1752), *Ehon nukumedori* (an erotic work), and *Ehon kin-echō* (an erotic work).

THE TWO-COLOR PRINT

The application by hand of colors, brass powder, and "lacquer" (ink mixed with glue), while beneficial to the print trade throughout

Kyōhō (1716–36) and Gembun (1736–41), was in the end too slow and costly a process to be commercially viable. No doubt Edo publishers felt the need to increase efficiency and profits, to improve upon their *modus operandi*. This led them to produce prints with block-printed colors, a technique that was to revolutionize ukiyo-e printmaking. The new technique was simply to carve in relief a right-angled mark at one lower corner and a short straight mark near the other lower corner of both the key block and color blocks. Accuracy of register was achieved by lining up the paper with these guide-marks, known as *kentō*.

According to an Edo-period record entitled *Bunruisan*, Sekine Shimbei was the first to devise these guide-marks. This is at variance with the prevalent view, as expressed by Shokusanjin (Ōta Nampo), that the publisher Uemura Kichiemon III of the Emi-ya, located at Shimmei-mae in Shiba, invented the *kentō*, enabling him to issue the first color prints in 1744. Apart from the invention of the guide-marks, it appears that the introduction and commercialization of color prints in ukiyo-e may be credited to Uemura, but the invention of the *kentō* could not have been his, because color printing existed in Japan long before 1744.[68]

At the beginning, the printing was done in only two colors: a rose-red (*beni*) and a soft green (*moegi*), in addition to the basic outline in black (*sumi*) originating from the key block. These two-color prints, called *benizuri-e*, were initially produced in the *hosoban* format. A third color could be created by means of printing the *beni* over the *moegi*, or vice versa, and a wide range of tones could be obtained by thinning or thickening the two dyes with which the color blocks were charged. In the 1750s this dichromatic palette was expanded to include colors such as yellow, gray, and blue. Furthermore, the application of *gaufrage* or embossing—a device later borrowed with much success by Harunobu—was yet another resource at the disposal of the artist.

If Masanobu could not pride himself on being the originator of the *benizuri-e*, he certainly was among the first exponents of the new technique. In any case, the Okumura-ya, as a competitive enterprise, had probably no other choice but to follow the lead taken by the Emi-ya in the field of the two-color print.

In spite of the enormous output of the print trade, surviving specimens of early *benizuri-e* in a good state of preservation are rather rare. The reason for this rarity is twofold. On the one hand, the vegetable dyes used in two-color prints were extremely fugitive; on the other hand, the paper on which these *hosoban* were printed was often of poor quality.

Figure 32, an uncut *hosoban* triptych on the theme of the courtesans of the three capitals that was introduced by Masanobu at the end of the Genroku epoch, shows the damaging effect of sunlight on unstable dyes, particularly on the rose-red (*beni*). Each of the three *hosoban* contains an ode, alas now reduced to illegible traces of faded *beni*. This defect notwithstanding, the embossing on the luxurious patterns of the kimono and the excellent draftsmanship contribute to make this fragile sheet of paper a prime example of early *benizuri-e*. In plate 29, an elegant portrait of Onoe Kikugorō I in the role of Sukeroku, Masanobu arrests our attention through his delicate lines and by his unexpected use of dark blue, which, superimposed on the *beni*, enables him to create the distinctive purple color of the actor's headband. The effective treatment of Sukeroku's intricate kimono design and, above all, the feeling for color harmony are the principal features of this gemlike print. It may be singled out as one of the most important works in the medium of two-color prints.

MASANOBU'S LAST YEARS: THE HŌREKI ERA

The application of colors by impression from woodblocks did not put an abrupt end to the hand-colored print. For a period of about six or seven years, or more precisely from 1744 to the dawn of the Hōreki era (1751–64), the *hosoban* hand-painted lacquer print coexisted, so to speak, with the *hosoban* block-printed two-color print (*benizuri-e*). That the art of color printing took so long to prevail over hand-coloring can be explained by the fact that the significance of the new technique, especially during its infancy, was not immediately perceived by the buying public. It seemed for a while that the lowly two-color print had less to offer than the more elaborate, fully-colored, brush-painted print.

The introduction of a third color block—a feeble attempt to enlarge the palette of the artist—did not really advance the basic color scheme inherent to the dichromatic *benizuri-e*. Some other improvement, some added feature had to be brought in to compensate for its obvious inadequacies.

Who else but Masanobu could give ukiyo-e the indispensable *élan* so vital to an art constantly subjected to the vagaries of momentary fashion and fads. The dichromatism of the *benizuri-e* demanded not' only a very skillful management of the colors employed, but also the creation of designs and dress patterns most apt to harmonize with the color distribution. In this respect, the frequent use of small checks on kimono (late 1740s and early 1750s) and *moiré* (starting from the mid 1750s), after the fashion of the day, helped the artist achieve compositional effects favorable to the two-color print. And if, because of its dimensions, the *hosoban* limited Masanobu's artistic vision, this limitation could be circumvented by producing works on a larger scale. Thus came into existence, at the beginning of Hōreki, the large *ōban* two-color print (about 43 by 31 cm.), a new format which allowed him to give full scope to his imaginative genius.

In the words of James Michener, an eminent ukiyo-e connoisseur, "no print of this period existing today surpasses print 35" (reproduced here as plate 31), "whose color and condition are perfect and whose representation of the gay arsonist, Yaoya O-Shichi, is so appealing."[24] This large two-color print, executed in the grand manner, portrays the famous lovers Oshichi and Kichisaburō dressed in the costume of *torioi* (literally, "bird chasers"), or wandering minstrels on their way to the sacred shrine at Ise. She is strumming on a samisen while he is playing a *kokyū*. The drama *Tsūjin chimata Soga*, from which this memorable scene was depicted, is a variation on one of the innumerable plays derived from the saga of the legendary Soga brothers. It was staged at the Ichimura-za in 1750 and starred Nakamura Kiyozō as Oshichi and Onoe Kikugorō as Kichisaburō. In accordance with Kabuki tradition (cf. plate 7), the crest of Arashi Kiyosaburō (d. 1713) was worn by the actor who enacted the role of Oshichi. Another print (pl. 30), a fine *hosoban* two-color print from the early 1750s, shows the actor Nakamura Kiyozō (wearing his own crest) as Shimano Okan standing in front of the *torii* of the Yushima shrine. Other notable examples of perfection in the two-color print, done in the large *ōban* vertical format, are reproduced in figures 31, 34, and 35.

It is not surprising that the delicacy of feeling for color and line, so inseparably associated with the aesthetics of the two-color print, brought about a gradual softening of the ukiyo-e style. This tendency had won the favor of influential publishers of the period—such as the Emi-ya, Urokogata-ya, Iga-ya, Murata-ya, Maru-ya, Sakai-ya, Iwato-ya, and Take-ya—who induced the artists working for them to create fashionable designs *à la* Masanobu. To some extent, they were responding to public demand, but at the same time they were trying to emulate the Okumura-ya, their chief competitor in the publishing business.

ABUNA-E OR RISQUÉ PRINTS

The brushwork of the new style emphasized graceful rather than forceful lines, sweet and slender rather than bold and massive forms. These characteristics were particularly conspicuous in prints of seminude beauties which came in vogue at the start of the Hōreki era (1751–64). In these works—commonly referred to as *abuna-e* or risqué pictures—young women were depicted in various states of quasi-undress, their very loose summer clothing revealing "inadvertently" part of their naked flesh. Such pictures were of course not without precedent in the long history of Japanese graphics, but never before had their production been so large, and their popularity so great, as during the Hōreki era.

Plate 32 is perhaps one of the earliest specimens in this genre. Without any intent to capitalize on the indecent or the lewd, Masanobu has composed an *abuna-e* of fresh originality. To be sure, his figure has none of the voluptuousness of an Ingres odalisque, and her mien is a bit mischievous, if not capricious. But for all that, she has allure, and she has charm. And what could be more exhilarating than a refreshing pause on the verandah just after a hot bath in a cypress-wood tub?

THE LAST PRINTS

Up until the late 1750s, as he was stepping into his eighth decade, Masanobu continued to work with undiminished zeal. In the evening of his life, there is no flagging in his creativity, no vacillation in his technique, no sign of weakness in his art. Masanobu, the unrivaled master, still maintained the exquisite sense of draftsmanship he had perfected during the early 1740s. One even detects, for instance in plate 33 and figure 33, the verve and alacrity of a man half his age.

Plate 34, a *hosoban* two-color print, requires a word of explanation since it is more than the mere depiction of a girl accosting a would-be customer. Despite the depressing reality of an occupation which was—depending on the courtesan's rank—either glorified or vilified, Masanobu has interpreted with candor the human drama of the nightless city. It is also an eloquent demonstration of the touch of satire implicit in many of his works. The subject is based on the popular legend of Watanabe no Tsuna (here the man-about-town) and the demon (now disguised as a courtesan of the Ōmiya teahouse) who haunted the Rashōmon, a well-known city gate in Kyoto. The famous warrior's crest (heraldically, three stars and a stripe), adroitly placed in the decorative motif around the edge of the umbrella, provides the clue to this parody. According to the story, Watanabe subdued the demon by cutting off its arm, but the demon, disguised as an old woman, eventually retrieved the severed arm from the hero.

As early as the 1710s Masanobu had done, in the *ōban* black-and-white format, another version of this design, though admittedly *une oeuvre de jeunesse* that lacked the maturity and deep insight of the *hosoban* composition. The remarkable grouping of the two figures, such as only Masanobu could conceive, the playful guile of the temptress in sharp contrast with the coyness of the all-too-willing victim, generate an atmosphere of expectancy, the prelude to the oldest game in the world. Such an exceptional design must have been held in high regard by the Edo public, for it was pirated by Torii Kiyohiro around 1760, and borrowed again by Harunobu at the end of the 1760s.

This is Masanobu's last appearance as a print designer. After a long and fruitful career in which he outlived most of his rivals as well as his own pupils, he passed away in the spring of 1764, a solitary genius with a publishing house to keep his name alive (the Okumura-ya flourished until around the mid 1780s, far beyond the "primitive" period), but without a successor capable of perpetuating the mastery and uniqueness of Masanobu's style. Masanobu had thoroughly exhausted the possibilities of the two-color print, and the technical feats at the last stage of his career foreshadowed the inevitability of the full-color print. By coincidence, his death occurs on the eve of the popularization of the polychrome *nishiki-e* (literally, "brocade picture"), at the beginning of Meiwa (1764–72)—an era which opened a new page in the history of ukiyo-e.

MASANOBU'S PAINTINGS

A final word must be added on Masanobu's achievements as a painter. Like most of the print designers of the popular school, Masanobu also worked in the ukiyo-e painting tradition. Although at least one of his paintings is known to have been done in the late 1750s, it appears that he was especially active in this art form during Kyōhō (1716–36), at a time when Miyagawa Chōshun (1683–1753) made a name for himself as a painter of the urban scene and, in particular, of beautiful women. While his courtesans have neither the grace nor the warmth of those of Masanobu, his ability to express the stylishness of the Yoshiwara belles should not be underestimated. In comparison with the fairly large number of Chōshun's extant paintings, those by Masanobu are relatively rare. The few surviving specimens bearing his signature give ample proof that he was, like his fellow artist Chōshun, a superb colorist who clothed his figures in bright and fashionable silks. On the surface, there are some affinities between the two masters, but most of these should be dismissed on stylistic grounds.

Masanobu's paintings are typically the product of a print designer. With him, the accent is always on a marvelous interplay of linear rhythms—a skill which he no doubt acquired in sketching hundreds of single sheets, album series, and book illustrations. This characteristic seems absent in Chōshun's work, where all the emphasis is on refinement, resulting in an art that is occasionally tinged with mellifluous preciosity. In spirit, Masanobu was perhaps closer to Hanabusa Itchō (1652–1724) than to any other genre painter. Through the bent of their temperament, both artists had in common a sense of the satiric and the comic. They shared alike a flair for executing fanciful compositions imbued with liveliness, and for delivering their hidden message with elegance and wit.

The Masanobu paintings illustrated in plate 35 and figure 36 (both of them parodies on historical subjects) display those very qualities that we admire in Itchō. Furthermore, they exhibit Masanobu's perfect balance of line, his genuine talent for color, and of course his innate aestheticism. It is easy to imagine the masterpieces he might have produced had he devoted his whole attention to the art of painting. After all, Masanobu was indeed "the originator of one school of ukiyo-e, without equal."

Fig. 1. *Yoshiwara Courtesans.* Fig. 2. *Bedroom Scene.* Fig. 3. *Wakakusa Genji monogatari.*

Fig. 4. *Self-portrait.* Fig. 5. *Masanobu?*

Fig. 6. *The Actor Morita Kanya II.*

Fig. 7. *Ukiyo-e Fantasy.*

Fig. 8. *Rats in a Sumō Tourney.*

Fig. 9. *Ebisu Worship at the New Year.*

Fig. 10. *"Pillow-Pulling" Game.*

Fig. 11. *Joie de Vivre.*

Fig. 12. *Escapade.*

Fig. 13. *Distraction.*

Fig. 14. *Ushiwakamaru and Benkei.*

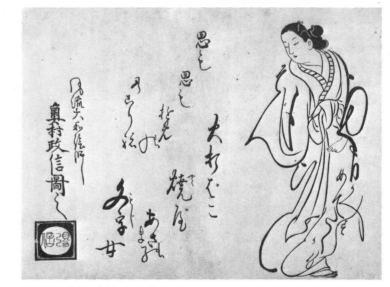

Fig. 15. *Calligraphic Tour de Force.*

Fig. 16. *The Playful Servant.*

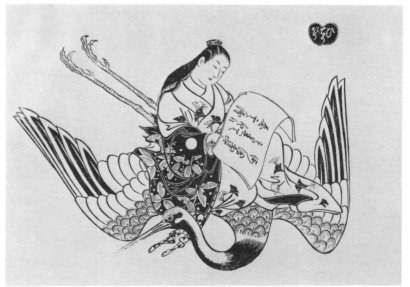

Fig. 17. *Magical Flight.*

Fig. 18. *Ichikawa Danjūrō II*, by Torii Kiyomasu.

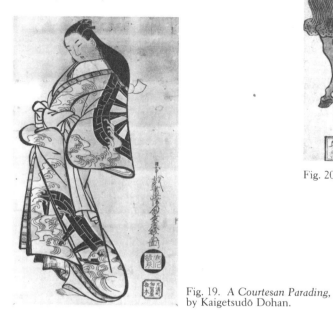

Fig. 20. *The Actor Ichikawa Monnosuke I.*

Fig. 19. *A Courtesan Parading*,
by Kaigetsudō Dohan.

Fig. 21. *Kabuki Scene.*

Fig. 22. *A Happy Trio.*

Fig. 23. *A Cock on a Jar of Rice.*

Fig. 24. *Night Rain at Karasaki.*

Fig. 25. *Chinese Sages.*

Fig. 26. *Lovers' Game.*

Fig. 27. *Lovers*, by Nishikawa Sukenobu.

43

Fig. 28. *Shōki.*

Fig. 29. *The Whisper.*

Fig. 30. *The Actor Ichikawa Ebizō I.*

Fig. 31. *Two Girls Going to the Theater.*

Fig. 32. *Courtesans of the Three Capitals.*

Fig.33. *Sanokawa Ichimatsu.*

Fig. 34. *The Maple Viewing Party.*

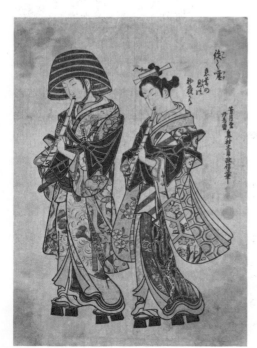

Fig. 35. *Mendicant Priests Playing the Flute.*

Fig. 36. *The Villa in Saga.*

Format	Approx. measurements (in centimeters)	Format	Approx. measurements (in centimeters)
kakemono-e tan-e	56 by 30	very large *ōban (uki-e)*	33 by 46
kakemono-e urushi-e	66 by 25	extra-large *ōban (uki-e)*	46 by 68
chūban sumizuri-e	20 by 30	narrow *hashira-e*	71 by 12
ōban sumizuri-e	26 by 38	*hashira-e*	71 by 15.5
large *ōban sumizuri-e*	29 by 43	extra-tall *hashira-e*	127 by 15.5
large *ōban benizuri-e*	43 by 31	*hosoban urushi-e* *hosoban benizuri-e*	30 by 15.5

Notes to the Illustrations

THE COLOR PLATES

Pl. 1. *Three Courtesans*. Ca. mid 1710s. *Kakemono-e tan-e*. Title (in cartouche): *Yūshoku sampukutsui* (A Triad of Beauties). Signature: Okumura Masanobu *zu* (Drawn by Okumura Masanobu). Seal: Masanobu. The kimono crests show that the courtesans represent the fair cities of Edo, Kyoto, and Osaka. Tobacco and Salt Museum, Tokyo.

Pl. 2. *A Courtesan Standing*. Ca. mid 1710s. *Kakemono-e tan-e*. Title (in cartouche): *Yūjo Chōkarō* (A Courtesan as Chōkarō). Signature: Okumura Masanobu *hitsu* (From the brush of Okumura Masanobu). Seal: Masanobu. Publisher: Asakusa Kiku-ya Komagata-chō (Kiku-ya at Komagata-chō in Asakusa). This is a parody on the Taoist sage Chōkarō, who had the magical power of producing a horse from a gourd. In this case, a courtesan has evoked a little pony (carrying a love letter) from a gourd-shaped netsuke. Courtesy of The Art Institute of Chicago.

Pl. 3. *A Courtesan Seated*. Ca. mid 1710s. *Kakemono-e tan-e*. Signature and seal: same as pl. 1. Publisher: Yushima Tenjin Komatsu-ya Onnazaka no Shita (Komatsu-ya near Yushima Tenjin Shrine at Onnazaka no Shita). Seated on a bench, a courtesan is pointing with her hairpin at a fan whose design consists of a pictorial puzzle (*hanjimono*). Courtesy of The Art Institute of Chicago.

Pl. 4. *A Courtesan Walking*. Ca. mid 1710s. *Kakemono-e tan-e*. Signature and seal: same as pl. 1. Publisher: Motohama-chō Iga-ya *hammoto* (Iga-ya in Motohama-chō, publisher). Courtesy of The Art Institute of Chicago.

Pl. 5. *An Iroko*. Early 1720s. *Hosoban urushi-e* with hand-coloring. Signature and publisher (in rectangular panel): *Nihon gakō Okumura Masanobu shōhitsu. Tōri Shio-chō edoiya beni-e ezōshi oroshi akaki hyōtan mejirushi tsukamatsuri sōrō Okumura* (From the genuine brush of the Japanese artist Okumura Masanobu. Offered by Okumura, the lacquer print and illustrated book wholesaler at the sign of the red gourd in Tōri Shio-chō). Gourd-shaped seal. Title (in circular cartouche): *Iroko, Ōsaka sampukutsui, u* (An Iroko Triptych, Osaka, Right [panel to viewer's left]). The inscription below the cartouche, which reads *Jō-jō-kichi* [superior superior excellence] *Sanokawa Mangiku*, refers to the performance grade of this actor, who was of exalted rank. This is a portrait of one of the female impersonators (*iroko*) of the three cities of Edo, Kyoto, and Osaka. Registered in Japan as an Important Art Object. [Reproduced in actual size.] Riccar Art Museum.

Pl. 6. *The Actor Ogino Isaburō*. Early 1720s. *Hosoban urushi-e* with hand-coloring. Inscription (top right): *Ganso* (The First) Ogino Isaburō. Signature and publisher (in rectangular panel): same as pl. 5. This is a depiction of Isaburō in the role of a handsome youth (*wakashu*). Registered in Japan as an Important Art Object. Riccar Art Museum.

Pl. 7. *Actor in the Role of Oshichi*. Ca. 1718. *Hosoban urushi-e* with hand-coloring. Signature: *Yamato gakō Okumura Masanobu hitsu* (From the brush of the Japanese artist Okumura Masanobu). Publisher: Sōshū[Sagami]-ya. This standing figure of an actor in a female role (*onnagata*) is presumably Sanjō Kantarō as Oshichi in the play *Keisei arashi Soga*, performed in 1718 at the Ichimura-za. According to Kabuki genealogical records (*Kabuki nendaiki*), the crest of Arashi Kiyosaburō was used by Kantarō in that very successful drama. [Reproduced in actual size.] Author's collection.

Pl. 8. *The Actor Ichikawa Danjūrō II*. 1726. *Hosoban urushi-e* with hand-coloring. Signature and publisher (in rectangular panel): *Nihon gakō ukiyo-e ichi-ryū kongen Okumura Shimmyō, rui nashi, Masanobu shōhitsu. Tōri Shio-chō ezōshi toiya akaki hyōtan shirushi Okumura-ya* (From the genuine brush of Masanobu, the unequaled Okumura Shimmyō, Japanese artist and founder of one school of ukiyo-e. The illustrated book wholesaler Okumura-ya at the sign of the red gourd in Tōri Shio-chō). Gourd-shaped seal. Scene from the play *Ōzakura ikioi Soga*, performed at the Nakamura-za in 1726. Author's collection.

Pl. 9. *The Actor Ichikawa Danjūrō II*. 1733. *Hosoban urushi-e* with hand-coloring. Signature and publisher (in rectangular panel): *Nihon gakō Okumura Masanobu hitsu ichi-ryū kongen. Tōri Shio-chō beni-e toiya* (From the brush of the Japanese artist Okumura Masanobu, the originator of one school of ukiyo-e. Lacquer print wholesaler in Tōri Shio-chō). Gourd-shaped seal. This print shows Danjūrō II as Soga no Gorō in the drama *Hanabusa bunjin Soga*, performed at the Nakamura-za in 1733. Courtesy of The Art Institute of Chicago.

Pl. 10. *Onnagata in Snow*. Ca. mid 1720s. *Hosoban urushi-e* with hand-coloring. Title (in vertical cartouche): *Shiki no kakiwake, yuki no ume* (Drawings of the Four Seasons: Plum Blossoms in Snow). Above the cartouche is the character *fuyu* (winter), but the top part has been trimmed off. Signature and publisher: *Ukiyo-e Nihon gakō Okumura Masanobu shōhitsu. Tōri Shio-chō beni toiya ezōshi oroshi akaki hyōtan mejirushi itashi sōrō Okumura-ya* (From the genuine brush of the Japanese ukiyo-e artist Okumura Masanobu. The Okumura lacquer print and illustrated book wholesaler at the sign of the red gourd in Tōri Shio-chō). Gourd-shaped seal. An unidentified *onnagata* (actor in female role), holding a dog in leash, takes a walk in the snow. [Reproduced in actual size.] Author's collection.

Pl. 11. *A Beautiful Woman Strolling*. Ca. mid 1720s. *Hosoban urushi-e* with hand-coloring. Signature and publisher: same as pl. 5. [Reproduced in actual size.] David Caplan Collection.

Pl. 12. *The Actor Tomisawa Montarō*. 1730s. *Hosoban urushi-e* with hand-coloring. Signature and publisher (in rectangular panel): same as pl. 8. [Reproduced in actual size.] Tobacco and Salt Museum, Tokyo.

Pl. 13. *The Moon of Musashi*. Ca. mid 1720s. *Hosoban urushi-e* with hand-coloring. Central sheet of a *Setsu-gekka* (Snow, Moon, Flower) triptych. Title (top right): *Musashi no tsuki, sampukutsui, chū* (The Moon of Musashi, a Triptych, Middle). Signature: *Nihon gakō Okumura Masanobu shōhitsu* (From the genuine brush of the Japanese artist Okumura Masanobu). Seal (in gourd): Okumura. Publisher (in circular cartouche): *Tōri Shio-chō kongen Okumura han. Kono hō no e nise-han sōrō aida hyōtan shirushi itashi sōrō* (Published originally by Okumura in Tōri Shio-chō. Since my prints are being spuriously published I put on the mark of the gourd). [Reproduced in actual size.] Bildarchiv Preussischer Kulturbesitz, Berlin.

Pl. 14. *Sparrows in the Snow*. Ca. mid 1720s. *Hosoban sumizuri-e* with hand-coloring. Signature and publisher: same as pl. 5. Courtesy of The Art Institute of Chicago.

Pl. 15. *A Paragon of Filial Piety*. 1720s. *Hosoban urushi-e* with hand-coloring. Title (in cartouche): *Nijūshi-kō, Kakkyo* (Twenty-four Paragons of Filial Piety: Kakkyo). Signature and publisher (across bottom): *Nihon gakō Okumura Masanobu shōhitsu. Tōri Shio-chō Okumura-ya* (From the genuine brush of the Japanese artist Okumura Masanobu. The Okumura publishing house in Tōri Shio-chō). Seal (in gourd): Okumura. Kakkyo thanks heaven for a miraculous stroke of fortune while his wife looks on. James A. Michener Collection. Honolulu Academy of Arts.

Pl. 16. *Lovers Watching a Handsome Youth Write*. Ca. mid 1730s. *Ōban sumizuri-e* with hand-coloring. Unsigned. The poem (left) reads: *Niō ume aun no kuchi no hatsu warai* (The fragant plum [the handsome youth] whose lovely mouth [brings] the first laugh of the year). Riccar Art Museum.

Pl. 17. *Teahouse Scene*. Early 1740s. Very large *ōban sumizuri-e* with hand-coloring. Title (top right): *Fūga hibachi muken no kane uki-e kongen* (An Original Perspective Print: The Elegant Brazier, Changing the Money). Signature (left): *Nihon tōbu gakō Hōgetsudō Tanchōsai Okumura Masanobu shōhitsu* (From the genuine brush of the Eastern Japanese artist Hōgetsudō Tanchōsai Okumura Masanobu). Publisher (bottom right): *Tōri Shio-chō akaki hyōtan shirushi Okumura-ya hammoto* (The publisher Okumura-ya at the sign of the red gourd in Tōri Shio-chō). Seal of the Wakai Collection. This is a parody on the tribulations of Umegae, a famous Osaka courtesan. Courtesy of The Art Institute of Chicago.

Pl. 18. *Enjoying the Evening Cool*. Early 1740s. Very large *ōban sumizuri-e* with hand-coloring. Title (top right): *Ryōgokubashi yūsuzumi uki-e kongen* (An Original Perspective Print: Enjoying the Evening Cool at Ryōgoku Bridge). Signature (left): *Tōbu Yamato gakō Hōgetsudō Tanchōsai Okumura Masanobu shōhitsu* (From the genuine brush of the Eastern Japanese artist Hōgetsudō Tanchōsai Okumura Masanobu). Publisher (bottom right): *Tōri Shio-chō hyōtan shirushi Okumura-ya Genroku hammoto* (The publisher Okumura-ya Genroku at the sign of the gourd in Tōri Shio-chō). Depicted here is the interior of a teahouse with courtesans and customers playing *sugoroku*, dancing, or just relaxing. Kobe City Museum.

Pl. 19. *Main Entrance to the Yoshiwara*. Early 1740s. Very large *ōban sumizuri-e* with hand-coloring. Title (top right): *Shin Yoshiwara ōmon-guchi*

Naka-no-chō uki-e kongen (An Original Perspective Print: The Main Gate and Naka-no-chō of the New Yoshiwara). Signature and publisher: same as pl. 17. In the foreground, the main thoroughfare of the Yoshiwara (Naka-no-chō) is seen swarming with people; in the background is a perspective view of the Tomoe-ya, one of the oldest teahouses of the Yoshiwara pleasure quarter. Tokyo National Museum.

Pl. 20. *Interior View of a Theater*. 1740. Extra-large *ōban sumizuri-e* with hand-coloring. Title (top right): *Shibai kyōgen butai kaomise ōuki-e* (Large Perspective Print of a Kabuki Drama and Comedy During a *Kaomise* Performance). Signature (left): *Edo-e ichi-ryū kongen* Hōgetsudō Tanchōsai Okumura Bunkaku Masanobu *shōhitsu* (From the genuine brush of the originator of one school of Edo-e [ukiyo-e], Hōgetsudō Tanchōsai Okumura Bunkaku Masanobu). Seal (in gourd): Tanchōsai. Publisher (bottom right): Tōri Shio-chō *etoiya akaki hyōtan shirushi* Okumura-ya Genroku *hammoto* (The publisher Okumura-ya Genroku, print wholesaler at the sign of the red gourd in Tōri Shio-chō). This print depicts the actor Ichikawa Ebizō as Yanone Gorō in the play *Miyabashira taiheiki*, performed at the Nakamura-za in 1740. Courtesy of The Art Institute of Chicago.

Pl. 21. *The Actor Sanokawa Ichimatsu I*. Ca. 1741. Extra-tall *hashira-e* with hand-coloring (*urushi-e*). Signature: Hōgetsudō Tanchōsai *hashira-e kongen* Okumura Bunkaku Masanobu *shōhitsu* (From the genuine brush of Hōgetsudō Tanchōsai Originator-of-the-Pillar-Print Okumura Bunkaku Masanobu). Seal: Tanchōsai. Courtesy of The Art Institute of Chicago.

Pl. 22. *Courtesan and Attendant*. Ca. mid 1740s. *Hashira-e* with hand-coloring (*urushi-e*). Signature: Hōgetsudō *shōmei hashira-e kongen* Okumura Bunkaku Masanobu *shōhitsu* (From the genuine brush of the authentic Hōgetsudō Originator-of-the-Pillar-Print Okumura Bunkaku Masanobu). Seal: Tanchōsai. The poem (top left) reads: *Yudan shite hana no kao miru aoba kana* (Being careless, the flowers I see, are they green leaves?). Museum of Fine Arts, Boston (Ross Collection).

Pl. 23. *Courtesan and Attendant*. Ca. mid 1740s. *Kakemono-e* with hand-coloring (*urushi-e*). Signature: Hōgetsudō *shōmei kongen* Okumura Bunkaku Masanobu *shōhitsu* (From the genuine brush of the authentic Hōgetsudō, the originator [of the pillar print], Okumura Bunkaku Masanobu). Seal and poem: same as pl. 22. Courtesy of The Art Institute of Chicago.

Pl. 24. *Courtesan and Attendant*. Ca. mid 1740s. *Kakemono-e* with hand-coloring (*urushi-e*). Signature, seal, and poem: same as pl. 23. This is an early impression (without the vertical break running from shoulder to heel on the standing figure) of the print in plate 23. Permission of The Fine Arts Museums of San Francisco.

Pl. 25. *Portrait of Shidōken*. Early 1740s. *Hashira-e* with hand-coloring. Title (in tablet): *Kosen monogatari kōshi Shidōken* (Shidōken, Lecturer in Tales of Ancient Battles). Signature: Hōgetsudō Okumura Bunkaku Masanobu *shōhitsu* (From the genuine brush of Hōgetsudō Okumura Bunkaku Masanobu). Seal: Tanchōsai. The poem (top left) reads: *Umi kaki wa Daruma no nari ya ketsu kusare* (An overripe persimmon, shaped like Daruma, with a rotten bottom). Author's collection.

Pl. 26. *The Actor Onoe Kikugorō I*. 1743. *Kakemono-e* with hand-coloring (*urushi-e*). Signature and seal: same as pl. 22. The poem (top right) reads: *Esugata o mite kazaritake sasara no oto ni Kikugorō* (Seeing his picture, beautiful sounds from bamboo sticks, Kikugorō). Depicted here is Kikugorō as Yoshino in the play *Haru no akebono kuruwa Soga*, performed at the Ichimura-za in 1743. Registered in Japan as an Important Art Object. Riccar Art Museum.

Pl. 27. *The Actor Onoe Kikugorō I*. 1744. *Kakemono-e* with hand-coloring (*urushi-e*). Signature: Hōgetsudō *shōmei* Okumura Bunkaku Masanobu *shōhitsu* (From the genuine brush of the authentic Hōgetsudō, Okumura Bunkaku Masanobu). Seal: Tanchōsai. The poem (top right) reads: *Ono ga ne no rembo no yami ya hototogisu* (With his own voice, in the darkness of love, the cuckoo). Kikugorō is shown here as Soga no Gorō in the play *Nanakusa wakayagi Soga*, performed at the Ichimura-za in 1744. Courtesy of The Art Institute of Chicago.

Pl. 28. *A Gust of Wind*. Ca. mid 1740s. *Kakemono-e* with hand-coloring (*urushi-e*). Signature and seal: same as pl. 25. The poem (top right) reads: *Suso e kaze ki no waruku naru haru no ame* (The wind in the folds of my dress . . . What a nuisance! Spring rain). A courtesan is taking a walk on a windy day. David Caplan Collection.

Pl. 29. *The Actor Onoe Kikugorō I as Sukeroku*. Late 1740s. *Hosoban benizuri-e*. Signature: Hōgetsudō Okumura Bunkaku Masanobu *ga* (Drawn by Hōgetsudō Okumura Bunkaku Masanobu). Seal: Tanchōsai. The poem (top left) reads: *Murasaki no musubu enishi o fujikazura*. Noguchi Yonejirō[37] translates this ode as follows: "How sweet is the affinity knot / In the purple band, / Nay, the purple vines of wisteria flowers!" Registered in Japan as an Important Art Object. Riccar Art Museum.

Pl. 30. *The Actor Nakamura Kiyozō as Shimano Okan*. Early 1750s. *Hosoban benizuri-e*. Signature and seal: same as pl. 29. The plaque (top left) on the *torii* shows the name of the shrine: Yushima Tenjingū. Tokyo National Museum.

Pl. 31. *Kabuki Scene*. 1750. Large *ōban benizuri-e*. Signature: Hōgetsudō Tanchōsai Okumura Bunkaku Masanobu *shōhitsu* (From the genuine brush of Hōgetsudō Tanchōsai Okumura Bunkaku Masanobu). Seal: Tanchōsai. The poem (top right) reads: *Koko mo Ise fudan-zakura ni ai no yama* (Here again in Ise where the cherry trees bloom, we meet with the mountain of

happiness). The actors Nakamura Kiyozō (in the female role) and Onoe Kikugorō I, respectively as Yaoya Oshichi and Kichisaburō, are dressed in the costumes of wandering minstrels. Museum of Fine Arts, Boston (Spaulding Collection).

Pl. 32. *After the Bath*. 1750s. Large *ōban benizuri-e*. Signature and seal: same as pl. 29. The poem (left) reads: *Ase ni naru tori ni rinki no fūfu tsure* (I perspire [but cover myself because] the hen is jealous of the rooster's distraction). Tokyo National Museum.

Pl. 33. *The Actor Takinaka Hidematsu*. Late 1750s. *Hosoban benizuri-e*. Title (bottom left): *Hanagasa sampukutsui* (Triptych of Beautiful Umbrellas). Signature: Hōgetsudō Okumura Masanobu *ga* (Drawn by Hōgetsudō Okumura Masanobu). Seals: Tanchōsai (in gourd) and Masanobu. The poem (top) reads: *Eda ni tsuku kashiku no ume ya fumi no tome* (The branch which bears the plum blossom, [shaped like] the salutation [the word *kashiku* written in cursive style] at the end of a letter). Takinaka Hidematsu was an early name of the actor Ichikawa Monnosuke II. Author's collection.

Pl. 34. *Teahouse Girl and Client*. Late 1750s. *Hosoban benizuri-e*. Signature: same as pl. 33. Seal: Tanchōsai. A girl of the Ōmiya teahouse, located in Naka-no-chō (the main street of the Yoshiwara licensed district), solicits a passer-by. Reproduced by Courtesy of the Trustees of the British Museum.

Pl. 35. *The Ogura Mountain Retreat*. 1720s. Painting on silk. Hanging scroll. Size: 32.1 by 48.5 cm. Signature: Okumura Masanobu *zu* (Painted by Okumura Masanobu). Seal: Masanobu. In the autumn rain a female warrior accompanied by an attendant holding a huge umbrella visits the mountain villa of a stylish nobleman. The characters on the plaque placed atop the porch indicate the location: Ogura Mountain. This is a parody on the love life of Fujiwara Sadaie, a nobleman of the Kamakura period, who is said to have compiled the *Hyakunin isshu* poetry anthology in his mountain retreat. Tokyo National Museum.

THE BLACK-AND-WHITE ILLUSTRATIONS

Fig. 1. *Yoshiwara Courtesans*. 1702. *Ōban sumizuri-e*. This is an album sheet from Masanobu's second signed work. The courtesans are Mandayū, whose hair is being combed by an attendant, and Komurasaki. Author's collection.

Fig. 2. *Bedroom Scene*. Book illustration in volume one of the *Wakakusa Genji monogatari* (1707) by Okumura Shimmyō Masanobu. Author's collection.

Fig. 3. Colophon in volume six of the *Wakakusa Genji monogatari* by Okumura Shimmyō Masanobu, showing the publication date (1707), the artist's signature, and the name and address of the publisher (Yamaguchi-ya Sansendō Sudō Gombei). Author's collection.

Fig. 4. *Self-portrait*. 1710s. *Ōban sumizuri-e*. This is the first sheet of an album of twelve comic prints published by Nishimura-ya. The inscription on the screen can be paraphrased as follows: "The painting of a hawk by Emperor Kisō as well as that of plum blossoms by Rinna are splendid, though perhaps too academic for the present day. When I showed such paintings to Okumura Masanobu and asked him how he would treat such subjects in the modern ukiyo-e style, he produced these pictures. Since they are not intended to be enjoyed alone, they have been engraved on wood for publication." If the date for this print is correct, and if Masanobu was born in 1686, he clearly looked, or caricatured himself to look, much older than a man aged twenty-four to thirty-three. Author's collection.

Fig. 5. *Masanobu?* 1710s. *Ōban sumizuri-e*. Title (in cartouche): *Yakko Chōryō* (Servant Chōryō). This is a parody on a legend about the Chinese hero Chōryō. When crossing a bridge over a certain river, Chōryō met an old man on a mule, who accidentally dropped one of his sandals into the stream. Chōryō plunged into the river and retrieved the sandal, whose owner turned out to be the famous sage Kōsekikō. As an indication of great strength, Chōryō is usually depicted standing on a dragon in the water. The characters *Masa* on the kimono of the samurai on horseback would suggest that the youth is Masanobu. Courtesy of The Art Institute of Chicago.

Fig. 6. *The Actor Morita Kanya II*. Ca. late 1700s. *Ōban sumizuri-e*. Signature: *Yamato eshi* Okumura Masanobu *zu* (Drawn by the Japanese artist Okumura Masanobu). Seal: Masanobu. Publisher: Nihombashi Minami Itchōme Yamaguchi-ya *shorin* Sudō Gombei (Yamaguchi-ya at Minami Ichōme in Nihombashi; bookstore of Sudō Gombei). The title of the print, *Shikata Nue* (The Way of the Nue), gives the clue to this farcical impersonation of the legendary archer Minamoto no Yorimasa, who killed the monster Nue. Courtesy of The Art Institute of Chicago.

Fig. 7. *Ukiyo-e Fantasy*. 1710s. *Ōban sumizuri-e*. This sheet belongs to the same comic series as figs. 4, 10–12. Like the Taoist immortal Chōkarō, who had the power of producing a horse from a gourd, three men, drawn in the *Toba-e* style, have evoked something much more to their fancy. Author's collection.

Fig. 8. *Rats in a Sumō Tourney*. Late 1700s. *Kakemono-e tan-e*. Signature: Okumura Masanobu *zu* (Drawn by Okumura Masanobu). Seal: Masanobu. Publisher: Motohama-chō Iga-ya *hammoto* (Iga-ya in Motohama-chō, publisher). Ōta Memorial Museum of Art.

Fig. 9. *Ebisu Worship at the New Year*. Ca. mid 1710s. *Kakemono-e tan-e*. Title (in cartouche): *Waka Ebisu omedetai* (Congratulations Young Ebisu). Signature, seal, and publisher: same as fig. 8. Courtesy of The Art Institute of Chicago.

Fig. 10. *"Pillow-Pulling" Game.* 1710s. *Ōban sumizuri-e.* Kimpira, the mythical strong man, plays "pillow-pulling" with a young girl, while her mistress looks on. Tokyo National Museum.

Fig. 11. *Joie de Vivre.* 1710s. *Ōban sumizuri-e.* Hotei, one of the seven gods of happiness, laughs at a book he is reading, while an *onnagata* (a Kabuki actor in a female role) plays the samisen. Courtesy of The Art Institute of Chicago.

Fig. 12. *Escapade.* 1710s. *Ōban sumizuri-e.* Signature: *Yamato eshi* Okumura Masanobu *zu* (Drawn by the Japanese artist Okumura Masanobu). Seal: Okumura Masanobu. Publisher: Nishimura *shimpan* (A new publication from Nishimura). Daruma, the Buddhist patriarch, and a courtesan have exchanged costumes; his fly whisk (a symbol of authority) is carried by the courtesan's attendant. Courtesy of The Art Institute of Chicago.

Fig. 13. *Distraction.* 1710s. *Ōban sumizuri-e.* Title (in cartouche): *Koi no kawa-fune Eguchi* (The Love Riverboat Eguchi). Priest Saigyō (the noted poet)—often depicted gazing at Mount Fuji—is distracted by a less lofty sight. As indicated in the cartouche, this print parodies the Noh play *Eguchi.* Courtesy of The Art Institute of Chicago.

Fig. 14. *Ushiwakamaru and Benkei.* 1710s. *Ōban sumizuri-e.* Signature: *Nihon eshi* Okumura Masanobu *zu* (Drawn by the Japanese artist Okumura Masanobu). Seal: Okumura Masanobu. Publisher: *Bukō* Nihombashi Minami Itchōme Yamaguchi-ya Gombei *hankō* (Published by Gombei of the Yamaguchi-ya at Minami Itchōme in Nihombashi, Edo). Here are depicted Ushiwakamaru (Minamoto no Yoshitsune), one of Japan's national heroes, and the giant Benkei, who became Yoshitsune's follower after an epic duel on Gojō Bridge. Riccar Art Museum.

Fig. 15. *Calligraphic Tour de Force.* Ca. mid 1710s. *Ōban sumizuri-e.* Signature: *Fūryū Yamato eshi* Okumura Masanobu *kore o zu su* (The elegant Japanese artist Okumura Masanobu drew this). Seal: Masanobu. The poems read: *Omoi mo omoi mo yume no nagorine* (Think, think of the traces of a dream); *Hiuchibako yaku ya asama no moji onna* (The flint box catches fire from the "letter-girl's" volatility). The outline of the courtesan's figure is made up of words used in feminine epistolary style. Courtesy of The Art Institute of Chicago.

Fig. 16. *The Playful Servant.* 1710s. *Ōban sumizuri-e.* A male servant (*wakamono*) tries to amuse his mistress while her two young female attendants (*kamuro*) play a prank on him. Although this print is unsigned, it can be safely attributed to Masanobu. Author's collection.

Fig. 17. *Magical Flight.* 1710s. Large *ōban sumizuri-e.* Title (in cartouche): *Hichōbō.* In lieu of the Taoist wizard Hichōbō, who had the power to ride on the back of a crane, Masanobu has substituted a courtesan. Worcester Art Museum, Worcester, Massachusetts.

Fig. 18. *The Actor Ichikawa Danjūrō II,* by Torii Kiyomasu I. 1710s. *Ōban sumizuri-e* with hand-coloring. Title (in cartouche): *Takenuki Gorō* (Gorō Uprooting a Bamboo). Signature: Torii Kiyomasu. Seal: Kiyomasu. Publisher: Motohama-chō Iga-ya *hammoto* (Iga-ya in Motohama-chō, publisher). Depicted here is the actor Ichikawa Danjūrō in the role of Soga no Gorō uprooting a bamboo tree. Ōta Memorial Museum of Art.

Fig. 19. *A Courtesan Parading,* by Kaigetsudō Dohan. Ca. mid 1710s. *Kakemono-e tan-e.* Signature: *Nihon giga* Kaigetsu *matsuyō* Dohan *zu* (An amusing picture in Japanese style, drawn by Dohan, a follower of Kaigetsu). Seal: Dohan. Publisher: Motohama-chō Iga-ya *hammoto* (Iga-ya in Motohama-chō, publisher). Registered in Japan as an Important Art Object. Tokyo National Museum.

Fig. 20. *The Actor Ichikawa Monnosuke I.* 1723. *Hosoban urushi-e* with hand-coloring. Signature, publisher, and seal: same as pl. 5. Scene from the drama *Hachi no ki onna mikyōsho,* performed at the Ichimura-za in 1723, in which Monnosuke played the role of Hōjō Tokimune. James A. Michener Collection. Honolulu Academy of Arts.

Fig. 21. *Kabuki Scene.* 1729. *Hosoban urushi-e* with hand-coloring. Signature, publisher, and seal: same as pl. 8. The actors Ichimura Takenojō and Sanokawa Mangiku (in the female role) in the play *Chōseiden hakuhatsu Kintoki,* performed at the Ichimura-za in 1729. Tokyo National Museum.

Fig. 22. *A Happy Trio.* Ca. mid 1720s. *Hosoban urushi-e* with hand-coloring. Title (top left): *Haori Daruma, waki sampukutsui, chū* (The Daruma Overcoat, A Happy Trio, Middle). Signature: Okumura Masanobu *shōhitsu* (From the genuine brush of Okumura Masanobu). Seal (in gourd): Okumura. Publisher (in circular cartouche): Tōri Shio-chō *kongen* Okumura *hammoto. Kono hō no e nise-han sōrō aida hyōtan shirushi itashi sōrō* (Published originally by Okumura in Tōri Shio-chō. Since my prints are being spuriously published I put on the mark of the gourd). Courtesy of The Art Institute of Chicago.

Fig. 23. *A Cock on a Jar of Rice.* Ca. mid 1720s. *Hosoban urushi-e* with hand-coloring. Signature: *Nihon gakō* Okumura Masanobu *shōhitsu* (From the genuine brush of the Japanese artist Okumura Masanobu). Gourd-shaped seal. Courtesy of The Art Institute of Chicago.

Fig. 24. *Night Rain at Karasaki.* Ca. late 1720s. *Hosoban urushi-e* with hand-coloring. Title (in gourd-shaped cartouche): *Karasaki no yau* (Night Rain at Karasaki). Signature (across bottom): same as fig. 23. The verse (top left) reads: *Yo no ame ni oto o yuzurite yūkaze o yoso ni nadatsuru Karasaki no matsu* (The night rain quells all sounds. Impervious to the night wind stands

the famous Karasaki pine). This is the first print in Masanobu's *Ōmi hakkei* (Eight Views of Lake Biwa). On a promontory of Lake Biwa a small temple is sheltered under the celebrated pine tree. H. M. Kaempfer Collection.

Fig. 25. *The Chinese Sages Kanyu and Tanfu.* Ca. late 1730s. *Hosoban ishizuri-e.* Signature (left): Hōgetsudō Okumura Masanobu *ga* (Drawn by Hōgetsudō Okumura Masanobu). Seal (in gourd): Tanchōsai. James A. Michener Collection. Honolulu Academy of Arts.

Fig. 26. *Lovers' Game.* 1720s. *Ōban sumizuri-e.* This is the cover sheet of an erotic album depicting the amusements in the nightless cities of Edo, Kyoto, and Osaka. A courtesan and her paramour play checkers with silver coins, utilizing the cross-lined pattern of the man's garment as a chessboard. James A. Michener Collection. Honolulu Academy of Arts.

Fig. 27. *Lovers,* by Nishikawa Sukenobu. Late 1710s. *Ōban sumizuri-e* with hand-coloring. Erotic album sheet. Author's collection.

Fig. 28. *The Demon Queller Shōki.* Ca. mid 1740s. Narrow *hashira-e* with washes of black ink (*urushi-e*). Signature: Hōgetsudō Tanchōsai Okumura Bunkaku Masanobu Baiō *ga* (Drawn by Hōgetsudō Tanchōsai Okumura Bunkaku Masanobu Baiō). Seal: Tanchōsai. Author's collection.

Fig. 29. *The Whisper.* Ca. mid 1740s. *Kakemono-e* with hand-coloring (*urushi-e*). Signature: Hōgetsudō *shōmei* Okumura Bunkaku Masanobu *shōhitsu* (From the genuine brush of the authentic Hōgetsudō, Okumura Bunkaku Masanobu). Seal: Tanchōsai. A seated courtesan has put her left arm around the shoulders of an attendant holding a love letter. Ōta Memorial Museum of Art.

Fig. 30. *The Actor Ichikawa Ebizō I.* 1749. *Kakemono-e* with hand-coloring (*urushi-e*). Signature: Hōgetsudō *hashira-e kongen* Okumura Bunkaku Masanobu *shōhitsu* (From the genuine brush of Hōgetsudō Originator-of-the-Pillar-Print Okumura Bunkaku Masanobu). Seal: Tanchōsai. This print depicts Ebizō as Sukeroku in the play *Otokomoji Soga monogatari,* performed at the Nakamura-za in 1749. The poem (top left) reads: *Wakayagite ebira no ume ya nido no kake* (Become young again! Arrows of plum branch, the second youth). Tokyo National Museum.

Fig. 31. *Two Girls Going to the Theater.* 1750s. Large *ōban benizuri-e.* Signature: Hōgetsudō Tanchōsai Okumura Bunkaku Masanobu *ga* (Drawn by Hōgetsudō Tanchōsai Okumura Bunkaku Masanobu). Seals: Tanchōsai (in gourd) and Masanobu. The poem (at top) reads: *Hikizome ya omou shibai-e shinobi-goma* (The first tune of the year . . . Pictures of actors we pine for . . . Just muted sounds). Accompanied by a boy carrying a samisen box, two girls are on their way to see a play. Reproduced by Courtesy of the Trustees of the British Museum.

Fig. 32. *Courtesans of the Three Capitals.* Late 1740s. Unsevered *hosoban benizuri-e* triptych, with embossing on kimono patterns. Title of set (in cartouche): *Sanga no tsu keisei, sampukutsui* (Courtesans of the Three Capitals: A Triptych). Inscriptions alongside cartouches: at the right, *Sa Ōsaka kakiwake* (Left: Osaka Design); in the center, *Chū Kyō kakiwake* (Middle: Kyoto Design); at the left, *U Edo kakiwake* (Right: Edo Design). Signature (on each panel): *Shōmei* Hōgetsudō Okumura Bunkaku Masanobu *ga* (Drawn by the authentic Hōgetsudō Okumura Bunkaku Masanobu); on central panel, *shōhitsu* (from the genuine brush of) in lieu of *ga* (drawn by). Seal (in gourd): Tanchōsai. Signature and publisher (on right panel only): *Edo-e ichi-ryū ganso* Hōgetsudō Tanchōsai Okumura Bunkaku Masanobu *shōhitsu. Shōmyō* Tōri Shio-chō Okumura-ya Genroku *hammoto* (From the genuine brush of Hōgetsudō Tanchōsai Okumura Bunkaku Masanobu, founder of one school of Edo-e [ukiyo-e]. The authentic publisher Okumura-ya Genroku in Tōri Shio-chō). Courtesy of The Art Institute of Chicago.

Fig. 33. *The Actor Sanokawa Ichimatsu I as Uga no Rangikumaru.* 1756. *Hosoban benizuri-e.* Signature and seal: same as pl. 29. Title (in cartouche): *Masakado shōzoku no enoki,* a play that was performed at the Nakamura-za in 1756. James A. Michener Collection. Honolulu Academy of Arts.

Fig. 34. *The Maple Viewing Party.* 1750s. Large *ōban benizuri-e.* Signature: same as fig. 31. Seals: Tanchōsai (in gourd) and Okumura Masanobu. The poem (top left) reads: *Irozuku ya momiji o taite sake no kan* (Glowing are the maple leaves that burn under the sake kettle). Three girls masquerading as imperial guards hold a party to admire the colors of the autumn leaves. The Metropolitan Museum of Art (Harris Brisbane Dick Fund, 1949).

Fig. 35. *Mendicant Priests Playing the Flute.* 1750s. Large *ōban benizuri-e.* Signature: same as pl. 31. Seal: Tanchōsai (in gourd). The poem (top right) reads: *Tsurete fuku rembo no iki no hatsu ne kana* (Playing the flute together with the breath of love. Their first affair?). Two lovers in disguise are taking a stroll. Worcester Art Museum, Worcester, Massachusetts.

Fig. 36. *The Villa in Saga.* 1720s. Painting on silk. Hanging scroll. Size: 32.1 by 48.5 cm. Signature: *Tōbu Yamato eshi* Okumura Masanobu *zu* (Painted by the Eastern Japanese artist Okumura Masanobu). Seal: Masanobu. Another autumn scene forming a pair with pl. 35. A stylish young man on horseback accompanied by three servants finds the mountain retreat of his paramour, guided by the sounds of a Japanese harp (*koto*) which she is playing. This is a parody on the love affair of Emperor Takakura (reigned 1169–80) and his favorite mistress Kōgo no Tsubone, who for reasons of state was forced into hiding. Under the full moon of an autumn night, the emperor sent out an old courtier to search for her, convinced that she would be playing a melody of love on the *koto.* His premonition proved to be true: she was found with her musical instrument near the capital, in the hills of Saga.

Selected Bibliography

1. Austin, James B. *Eight Hundred Years of Japanese Printmaking*. Pittsburgh: Museum of Art, Carnegie Institute, 1976.

2. Azechi, Umetarō. *Japanese Woodblock Prints: Their Techniques and Appreciation*. English translation by Charles A. Pomeroy. Rutland, Vt., and Tokyo: Japan Publications, 1963.

3. Binyon, Laurence. *A Catalogue of Japanese and Chinese Woodcuts Preserved in the Sub-department of Oriental Prints and Drawings in the British Museum*. London: The Trustees of the British Museum, 1916.

4. Binyon, Laurence, and Sexton, J. J. O'Brien. *Japanese Colour Prints*. London: Ernest Benn, 1923. 2nd edition, ed. Basil Gray. London: Faber and Faber, 1960. Reprinted, London: Robert G. Sawers Publishers, 1978.

5. Boxer, C. R. *Jan Compagnie in Japan, 1600–1817: An Essay on the Cultural, Artistic and Scientific Influence Exercised by the Hollanders in Japan from the Seventeenth to the Nineteenth Centuries*. The Hague: Martinus Nijhoff, 1950 (2nd rev. ed.). Reprinted, Tokyo: Oxford University Press, 1968.

6. Fenollosa, Ernest F. *The Masters of Ukioye. A Complete Historical Description of Japanese Paintings and Color Prints of the Genre School Shown in Exhibition at the Fine Arts Building*. New York: W. H. Ketcham, 1896.

7. Fenollosa, Ernest F. *An Outline of the History of Ukiyo-ye*. Tokyo: Kobayashi Bunshichi, 1901.

8. Ficke, Arthur D. *Chats on Japanese Prints*. London and New York: T. Fisher Unwin, 1915. Reprinted, Rutland, Vt., and Tokyo: Tuttle, 1958.

9. Fujikake, Shizuya. *Ukiyo-e no kenkyū*. 3 vols. Tokyo: Nihon Shuppan Haikyū, 1943.

10. Gookin, Frederick W. "Okumura Masanobu's *Yamato Irotake*" (in *Eastern Art*, vol. 1, no. 1). Philadelphia, 1928.

11. Gunsaulus, Helen C. *The Clarence Buckingham Collection of Japanese Prints: The Primitives*. Chicago: The Art Institute of Chicago, 1955.

12. Henry, Charles Arsène. "Tapisseries et Soieries Japonaises" (in *Bulletin de la Maison Franco-Japonaise*, Tome 12, no. 1). Paris and Tokyo, 1941.

13. Hillier, J. *The Japanese Print: A New Approach*. Rutland, Vt., and Tokyo: Tuttle, 1960.

14. Inoue, Kazuo. "Okumura Masanobu ni kansuru sensaku" (in *The Ukiyoe no Kenkyu*, vol. 5, no. 3). Tokyo, 1926.

15. Inoue, Kazuo. *Ukiyo-eshi den*. Tokyo: Watanabe Hangaten, 1931.

16. Jenkins, Donald. *Ukiyo-e Prints and Paintings: The Primitive Period, 1680–1745. An Exhibition in Memory of Margaret O. Gentles*. Chicago: The Art Institute of Chicago, 1971.

17. Kikuchi, Sadao. *Ukiyo-e Prints*. English translation by Don Kenny. Tokyo: Tokyo International Publishers, 1970.

18. Kobayashi, Tadashi. *Ukiyo-e*. English translation by Mark A. Harbison. Tokyo and New York: Kodansha International, 1982.

19. Lane, Richard. *Masters of the Japanese Print*. London and New York: Thames and Hudson, 1962.

20. Lane, Richard. *Images from the Floating World (Including an Illustrated Dictionary of Ukiyo-e)*. New York: Putnam, 1978.

21. Ledoux, Louis V. *Japanese Prints of the Ledoux Collection*. 5 vols. New York: E. Weyhe (vols. 1–3), and Princeton University Press (vols. 4–5), 1942–51.

22. Link, Howard A. *The Theatrical Prints of the Torii Masters*. Tokyo: Riccar Art Museum, and Honolulu: Honolulu Academy of Arts, 1977.

23. Link, Howard A. (with the assistance of Suzuki Jūzō and Roger S. Keyes). *Primitive Ukiyo-e from the James A. Michener Collection in the Honolulu Academy of Arts*. Honolulu: The University Press of Hawaii, 1980.

24. Michener, James A. *The Floating World*. New York: Random House, 1954.

25. Michener, James A. *Japanese Prints from the Early Masters to the Modern*. With notes on the plates by Richard Lane. Rutland, Vt., and Tokyo: Tuttle, 1959.

26. Mitchell, C. H., Narazaki, M., et al. "An Exhibition of Masterpieces of Ukiyo-e by the Japan Ukiyo-e Society" (in *Ukiyo-e Art*, vol. 3). Tokyo, 1963.

27. Mitchell, C. H. (with the assistance of Ueda Osamu). *The Illustrated Books of the Nanga, Maruyama, Shijo and Other Related Schools of Japan, a Biobibliography*. Los Angeles: Dawson's Book Shop, 1972.

28. Miyao, Shigeo. *Nihon no giga: Rekishi to fūzoku*. Tokyo: Daiichi Hōki Shuppan, 1967.

29. Miyatake, Gaikotsu. *Okumura Masanobu gafu*. Osaka: Gazoku Bunko, 1910.

30. Nakada, Katsunosuke. *Ehon no kenkyū*. Tokyo: Bijutsu Shuppansha, 1950.

31. Narazaki, Muneshige. *The Japanese Print: Its Evolution and Essence*. English adaptation by C. H. Mitchell. Tokyo and New York: Kodansha International, 1966.

32. Narazaki, Muneshige. *Studies in Nature: Hokusai—Hiroshige*. English translation by John Bester. Tokyo and New York: Kodansha International, 1970.

33. Netto, C., and Wagener, G. *Japanischer Humor*. Leipzig: F. A. Brockhaus, 1901.

34. *Nihon hanga bijutsu zenshū*. 8 vols. Tokyo: Kōdansha, 1960–62.

35. Nihon Sembai Kōsha. *Ukiyo-e to kitsuengu*. Tokyo: Tobacco and Salt Museum, 1967.

36. Noguchi, Yonejirō. *Roku dai ukiyo-eshi* (final ed.). 6 vols. Tokyo: Seibundō, 1932.

37. Noguchi, Yone. *The Ukiyoye Primitives*. Tokyo: privately published, 1933.

38. Ōta Memorial Museum of Art. *Inaugural Exhibition Catalogue of Ukiyo-e Prints*. Tokyo, 1980.

39. Paine, Robert Treat, Jr. "Some Pillar Prints by Masanobu" (in *Bulletin of the Museum of Fine Arts*, vol. 57, no. 308). Boston, 1959.

40. Paine, Robert Treat. "Japanese Prints of Birds and Flowers by Masanobu and Shigenaga" (in *Oriental Art*, n.s. vol. 9, no. 1). London, 1963.

41. Paine, Robert Treat. "The Masanobu Tradition of Courtesans of the Three Cities" (in *Ars Orientalis*, vol. 5). Baltimore, Md., 1963.

42. Sansom, G. B. *Japan: A Short Cultural History*. London: Cresset Press, 1931.

43. Sansom, G. B. *The Western World and Japan*. New York: Alfred A. Knopf, 1962.

44. Schmidt, Steffi. *Katalog der chinesischen und japanischen Holzschnitte im Museum für Ostasiatische Kunst*. Berlin: Bruno Hessling, 1971.

45. Sekine, Shisei. *Meijin kishin roku*. Tokyo: Yoshikawa Hanshichi, 1894. 2nd edition, ed. Sekine Masanao, Tokyo, 1929. Reprinted, Tokyo: Yumani Shobō, 1977.

46. Shibui, Kiyoshi. *Genroku ko-hanga shūei. Estampes Erotiques Primitives du Japon*. 2 vols. Tokyo: privately published, 1926–28.

47. Shibui, Kiyoshi. "Masanobu no sumi-e" (in *The Ukiyoye no Kenkyu*, vol. 6, no. 3). Tokyo, 1929.

48. Shibui, Kiyoshi. *Ukiyo-e Naisi*. 2 vols. Tokyo: Taihōkaku Shobō, 1932–33.

49. Shibui, Kiyoshi. *Shoki hanga*. Tokyo: Asoka Shobō, 1954.

50. Shibui, Kiyoshi. "Proto-Tokyo" (in *Ukiyo-e Art*, vol. 8). Tokyo, 1964.

51. Stern, Harold P. *Master Prints of Japan*. New York: Harry N. Abrams, 1969.

52. Suzuki, Jūzō. *Nihon hanga benran* (supplement to *Nihon hanga bijutsu zenshū*). Tokyo: Kōdansha, 1962.

53. Suzuki, Susumu. *Masterworks of Ukiyoe from the Hiraki Collection*. Tokyo: Riccar Art Museum, 1964.

54. Takahashi, Seiichirō. *Traditional Woodblock Prints of Japan*. English translation by Richard Stanley-Baker. New York and Tokyo: Weatherhill, 1972.

55. Tokyo National Museum. *Illustrated Catalogues of the Tokyo National Museum—Ukiyo-e Prints*. 3 vols. Tokyo, 1960–63.

56. Toyama, Usaburō. *The Western-style Colour Prints in Japan*. Tokyo: Daiichi Shobō, 1936.

57. *Ukiyo-e shūka*. 16 vols. Tokyo: Shōgakkan, 1978–82.

58. *Ukiyo-e taika shūsei*. 20 vols. Tokyo: Taihōkaku Shobō, 1931–32.

59. *Ukiyo-e taisei*. 12 vols. Tokyo: Tōhō Shoin, 1930–31.

60. *Ukiyo-e zenshū*. 6 vols. Tokyo: Kawade Shobō, 1956–58.

61. van Rappard-Boon, C. (with the assistance of Roger S. Keyes and Keiko Keyes-Mizushima). *Catalogue of the Collection of Japanese Prints in the Rijksprentenkabinet. Part I: The Age of Harunobu*. Amsterdam: Rijksmuseum, 1977.

62. Vergez, Robert. "The Early Prints of Okumura Masanobu" (in *Ukiyo-e Art*, vol. 42). Tokyo, 1974.

63. Vergez, Robert. "Masanobu's *Ehon Ogura Nishiki*" (in *Ukiyo-e Art*, vol. 48). Tokyo, 1975.

64. Vergez, Robert. "Okumura Genroku, Artist and Publisher" (in *Ukiyo-e Art*, vol. 49). Tokyo, 1976.

65. Vignier, Charles, and Inada, H. *Estampes Japonaises Exposées au Musée des Arts Décoratifs*. 4 vols. Paris, 1909–12. Reprinted, Geneva: Minkoff, 1973.

66. Vignier, Charles; Lebel, J.; and Inada, H. *Estampes Japonaises Exposées au Musée des Arts Décoratifs*. 2 vols. Paris, 1913–14. Reprinted, Geneva: Minkoff, 1973.

67. Volker, T. *Ukiyo-e Quartet: Publisher, Designer, Engraver, and Printer*. Leyden: E. J. Brill, 1949.

68. Waterhouse, D. B. *Harunobu and His Age: The Development of Colour Printing in Japan*. London: The Trustees of the British Museum, 1964.

69. Waterhouse, David. *Images of Eighteenth-Century Japan*. Toronto: Royal Ontario Museum, 1975.

70. Yoshida, Teruji. *Ukiyo-e jiten*. 3 vols. Tokyo: Gabundō, 1971.

定価3,700円
in Japan